THE UNIVERSITY OF WEST FLORIDA
3 2100 0021 4 96 2

AF361169

Freedom: Reason or Revolution?

Freedom
Reason or Revolution?

Edited by

Gordon Bowker
*Lecturer in Sociology, Goldsmiths' College,
University of London*

Routledge & Kegan Paul

First published 1970
by Routledge & Kegan Paul Ltd
Broadway House, 68–74 Carter Lane
London, E.C.4
Printed in Great Britain
by Cox & Wyman Ltd, London,
Fakenham and Reading
© Gordon Bowker 1970

SBN 7100 6749 6 (L)
SBN 7100 6803 4 (C)

Contents

Acknowledgements

We should like to express our thanks for permission to use the following: R. S. Peters: *Authority, Responsibility and Education* (George Allen & Unwin Ltd.); G. B. Shaw: *The Apple Cart* (The Society of Authors, as Agent for the Bernard Shaw Estate); Michael Kullman: *The Anti-Culture Born of Despair* (New Left Review); J. A. C. Brown: *The Techniques of Persuasion* (Penguin Books Ltd.); Colin MacInnes: *Nicked* (New Society); James Baldwin: *The Fire Next Time* (Michael Joseph Ltd.); Henry Fairlie: *Martin Luther King* (Encounter); Raymond Williams: *Communication in the Sixties* (Penguin Books Ltd.); Kenneth Tynan: *Right and Left* (Longmans Green & Co. Ltd.); Vance Packard: *The Hidden Persuaders* (Longmans Green & Co. Ltd.); Jacob Bronowski: *The Commonsense of Science* (Heinemann Educational Books Ltd.); Richard Davy: *Distress over Modern Society* (Times Newspapers Ltd.); Patrick Seale and Maureen McConville: *French Revolution, 1968* (Penguin Books Ltd.); Tad Szulc (New York Times Co.).

Special thanks are due to the National Council for Civil Liberties for their free permission to use the pamphlet *Arrest* and to Mr Douglas Hyde whose article *The Pope and the Pill* was written specifically for this book.

Introduction

'Freedom' is a very attractive word and, in this age of protest and would-be revolution, a highly popular slogan. But it is a slogan which means different things to different people. For the American Negro it may mean freedom to live outside the ghettoes and enjoy the affluent living of modern America; for the civil rights demonstrator in Northern Ireland, freedom to have an equal say in his own government; for persecuted Soviet writers, freedom to publish their work without fear of imprisonment; for the young, freedom to enjoy a socially and sexually permissive life; for the student, freedom to have a greater say in what he studies; and for the anarchist, freedom from all society's laws and restrictions.

The anarchist would probably agree with Jean-Jacques Rousseau, the eighteenth-century French philosopher, who wrote 'Man is born free, and everywhere he is in chains'. By Rousseau's extremist argument it is society, its government, laws and conventions which enslave men. If these, and the police who enforce the laws, were to be abolished, all men would live together in freedom and harmony. At the other political extreme, the totalitarian, whether he is a Fascist or a Communist, believes that men are too violent and disorganized to be left to themselves and can only behave decently when subjected to tough laws ruthlessly enforced. For instance, Lenin, the Russian revolutionary leader, is reputed to have once said that 'Liberty is precious – so precious that it must be rationed'.

The democrat stands somewhere between these two extremes. He believes that, although governments are potentially evil, they are necessary. There must be laws to prevent the strong from exploiting the weak, but the power of those in authority must be carefully watched and restricted. As Wendell Phillips once said, 'Eternal vigilance is the price of liberty.' Of course, many people take their freedom for granted and are not always prepared to share the responsibility of fighting to preserve it. In fact not everybody is prepared to take responsibility for their own actions freely performed. (See Richard Peters on page 5.)

But 'democracy', like 'freedom', can mean different things to different people. The Russian Communists claim to have a democratic system of government, yet the voter has no choice but to vote for candidates approved by the Party. Democracy in Northern Ireland does not mean that everyone over twenty-one has a vote, whereas some have more than one. Are we, like the Russians, deluding ourselves when we say Britain is a democracy? (See Bernard Shaw, page 16.)

But even where a democracy exists which allows full participation of the people in their own government, freedom of speech, freedom to congregate, to protest, to go on strike, to worship, etc., those in authority may not always use their power for the benefit of all. Some people, for example, believe that the political and economic systems in Britain and the United States favour the rich – capitalists who own the means of production – and leave manual workers both impoverished and alienated from their work. (See Erich Fromm, page 29.)

According to John Stuart Mill, the nineteenth-century English philosopher, 'Liberty consists in doing what one desires.' But freedom to choose the kind of work one wants to do and the life one wants to live, depends more and more on education. Today there is greater educational opportunity in Britain than ever before. But is there enough? Many very clever children, especially those who come from working-class backgrounds, leave school early. One important reason for this, according to sociologists, is that they feel hostile to the middle-class culture of the school. Their freedom of choice in life is therefore being restricted by the very institutions which should be widening their horizons. (See Michael Kullman, page 47.)

Freedom to choose, not only one's job, but also where one can go and where one can live, is sometimes denied to individuals because of their race or the colour of their skin. This can happen even in the United States and Britain, which pride themselves on being both democratic and free. Abraham Lincoln often expressed the desire that all men everywhere should be free. But more than a hundred years after his death many American Negroes live in ghettoes, cooped up and denied the opportunities available to their white fellow-citizens. (See Henry Fairlie, page 98.)

One freedom the Negroes of America do enjoy is freedom to worship God in their own way. (See James Baldwin, page 86.) Religious freedom has been established in Britain, too, for many years now. But there was a time when many in this country saw the acceptance of the Pope's authority by Roman Catholics as a threat to the authority of the monarch and Parliament. This is the view still taken by many Protestants in Northern Ireland. Now, even inside the Roman Catholic Church itself, some of its members are feeling their freedom of conscience threatened by the same authority. (See Douglas Hyde, page 78.)

But whatever one's social status, race or religion, everyone in a democratic society is required to obey its laws. Some people see the law as indicating just how far one can go in pursuing a life of freedom. The French philosopher Montesquieu, for example, once defined liberty as 'the right to do what the laws allow.' Of course, not everyone agrees that all laws are just and ought to be obeyed. Nor does everyone trust the way in which the police enforce the laws. In some countries police use methods which would not be tolerated here. (See J. A. C. Brown, page 58.) In fact very strict rules are laid down in England and Wales which say just what the police can and cannot do to suspects. (See *Arrest*, page 64.) Even so, are these rules always obeyed? (See Colin MacInnes, page 72.)

Threats to men's freedom are not always a direct result of bad government or uncontrolled police action. They may arise out of some men abusing their freedom to exploit others. A French visitor to America in the 1820's wrote, 'Liberty here means to do each as he pleases, to care for nothing and nobody, and cheat everybody.' Many of the most blatant and damaging forms of exploitation have been eliminated in both the United States and Britain, but others, less obvious but perhaps just as harmful, have taken their place. For example, the mass media – Press, radio, television, advertising – are seen by some observers as being so influential and persuasive as to threaten our freedom of choice. (See Raymond Williams, page 107 and Vance Packard, page 124.) Others fear that an even greater threat is the freedom given to scientists to develop new techniques which could be used to create fearful new weapons of destruction. (See Jacob Bronowski, page 131.)

Views about freedom, then, are very varied and sometimes conflicting. It has been said that freedom is simply a state of mind, but for most writers on the subject freedom has depended very much on the way a society is run. This view is certainly held by radical students in most democratic industrial societies. To achieve their ideal of a better society, free of inequalities, they are often prepared to engage in open revolt (see Richard Davy, page 142 and Patrick Seale and Maureen McConville, page 148).

Oddly enough, in Czechoslovakia, where hard-won freedom was recently threatened by one of the world's greatest powers, the population chose passive rather than active resistance to defend their liberty (see Tad Szulc, page 172). The Czechs have had to fight for their freedom many times before. Perhaps they have learned that to secure and preserve freedom the battle must be fought in a very special way. Mahatma Gandhi, the modern pioneer of passive resistance, held the view that to use violence to gain freedom in India would only result in a violent Indian government replacing a violent British one. If the price of liberty is external vigilance, it is worth asking whether the best way to preserve and extend it is by peaceful means – by reason and persuasion – or by the more violent tactics of the perpetual revolutionaries.

It is hoped that this collection of articles and passages from biographies and scientific, sociological and psychological works will help to expand upon and perhaps to answer many of the questions raised in this Introduction. For the student of social and liberal studies, who may be using this as a course textbook, discussion points, suggestions for projects and further reading have been included.

Clearly this kind of anthology can be used by the student and teacher in a number of different ways. For example, it might be taken as the basis for a year-long course on Freedom and used in conjunction with other materials – reading-matter, films and television programmes. Such a course might involve visits to some of the agencies and institutions considered, e.g. a law court, a prison, a newspaper office, an advertising agency, a motor-car factory, etc. A second approach might be to use just one section of the book as a way into a study in depth of one of the topics considered, e.g. Race, The Mass Media, Revolution.

GORDON BOWKER

Richard Peters
Living without authority

from *Authority, Responsibility and Education,*
Allen & Unwin, 1959

Are men responsible for their actions, or are these determined by their past history? The rise of modern science, especially the human sciences such as psychology and sociology, have given modern man new insights into why people behave as they do. Thieves, say some psychologists, are really stealing love and are the products of broken homes; violent crimes are likely to be committed by individuals brought up in an atmosphere of family violence; many of the most sadistic Nazis were men whose ambitions in life had been frustrated. But how far can such *explanations* be taken as *excuses* for immoral or anti-social behaviour? Some of the fundamental issues connected with freedom and responsibility are considered in the following passage by Richard Peters, the philosopher, taken from his book, *Authority, Responsibility and Education*.

One of the most impressive changes that has come over our society in the past three hundred years has been a gradual one. It could be dramatically described as the rise of the fatherless society.

Up to the seventeenth century men were dominated by the figure of the father in all departments of life. In the family the father was a real patriarch and the sort of authority which he exerted over his children was mirrored in the authority of kings, bishops, lords, squires, and the Pope. Gradually, however, this patriarchal kind of authority has been passing away. Even in the face to face communities of the village and the small country town the squire and the vicar no longer meet with that total deference which was once their due. A more brotherly sort of society has grown up in which men take increasing responsibility for their own lives. Men rise in society more because of their ability than because of their birth, and women are not universally regarded as inferior simply because they are women.

This gradual change in people's attitudes is far more important than that brought about by any sudden revolution. But we are not finding it too easy. When we grow up and begin to stand on our own feet we often long for the security of our childhood days when our parents made all the decisions. It is the same with society. When things prove difficult it is only too easy to return to the father in the form of a dictator, as many have done. Then there is also a tendency to find a *new* sort of man to take on this ancient patriarchal role. The old religious or political leaders no longer cut much ice with most of us as authorities; we treat the doctor, who looks after our bodies, or the psychiatrist who looks after our minds, with much more respect than the priest who looks after our souls. And we have become so disillusioned with politicians that we treat them with a certain degree of derision. This increased respect for the doctor is symptomatic; for in the minds of many the scientist has stepped into the place from which old authorities have been ousted. After all, it is now the scientist rather than the priest who knows about the mysteries of life – things like space travel, reconstructing living cells out of chemicals, mechanical brains that may replace human ones, and the alarming contents of our unconscious minds. And it is the scientist rather than the politician who delivers the goods – television sets, refrigerators, soapless detergents and atomic bombs.

Many scientists seem only too glad to put on this mantle of authority. They make public pronouncements about peace and war; they mingle ethics with evolution and religion with astronomy; and, of course, our ears are ringing with scientific counsels about bringing up our children. The scientist in our community is in danger – and it *is* a danger – of becoming like Plato's philosopher king – not just an expert in a particular field of research like evolution or nuclear physics, but an expert on the good for society and for the individual. And how comforting for us to be able to pass on those tormenting problems about what we ought to do to the expert. Here is a new way of returning to the father, of exchanging the worries and responsibilities of adult life for the security of childhood, of staying mentally for ever in short trousers.

It is, indeed, rather ironical that the scientist should appear as a kind of authority. For science, like morality, is basically anti-authoritarian. And, as a matter of fact, the development of both science and morality are two of the most important features of the emergence of the more brotherly kind of society which has replaced the patriarchal sort.

A scientist, surely, is a man who acknowledges no authority. He gives up what is distinctive of his calling if he believes things just because somebody says that they are true. He believes that bodies fall at a certain rate to the ground not because Galileo or anyone else said so, but because the experiments can be performed which convince him that what Galileo said was true. In a scientific discussion it is essential to listen to the reasons a person gives for his beliefs and to ignore his personal or social oddities. We do not accept them just because they are *his* beliefs, or because he claims some kind of revelation or authority for them. Neither do we reject them just because we do not like the colour of his skin or his family connections. We must listen to the argument and ignore the man. This is what we call being reasonable or using our reason.

Of course some scientists come to be called 'authorities' on particular matters. But this only means that they have studied the subject closely and, in the past, have put forward theories that have been found to fit the facts. In the same way we speak of reliable witnesses. With such people there is a strong presumption that they are talking sense on certain topics, but only a strong presumption. They may, after all, be wrong on this occasion in spite of their reputation. And, of course, outside their own sphere their opinion is no better than that of any other reasonable man who has had a different sort of training. A training in physics or phonetics does not, of itself, produce political pundits.

Morality has the same anti-authoritarian character as science and it is no accident that the two have developed together. Now 'morality' does not mean just doing the done thing or performing duties required by a religious or civil authority. For then there would be no distinction between custom, religion, law, and morality. It means acting on a code that the individual has accepted as his own. We can believe that gambling is wrong just because we have been brought up that way. This is a matter of custom. Or we can believe that gambling is wrong because we have thought about it and seen that there are *reasons* against it. When somebody says to himself things like 'My parents say that birth-control is wrong, but I wonder whether it really is' he is beginning to accept or reject rules because he sees the *point* of them and not simply because somebody has laid them down.

This elucidation of the concept of 'morality' makes explicit why accepting anyone – including a scientist – as an authority on what ought to be done is incompatible with our moral responsibility. For if anyone accepts that he ought to do something just because a scientist tells him to, he is not making it part of his *moral* code. Of course, the scientist may give good reasons for his advice; but in that case his advice is being accepted because of the reasons which he gives rather than just because *he* gives it.

There is a further reason why it is especially incongruous to accept the scientist as an authority about what ought to be done in social and personal matters. His job is to classify and explain facts: what species flowers and plants belong to; why iron expands in the fire; or why our pipes freeze. But he only tells us what is the case and why it is so. He does not tell us what *ought* to be the case. A psychologist may tell us why children tend to steal, a social scientist about the causes of unemployment. But they cannot tell us as *scientists* that stealing or unemployment is *wrong*. Science is concerned with facts, morality with decisions about facts. So, though a scientist can help us to clear our minds about what the facts are and what has caused them, he cannot, as a scientist, tell us what we ought to do about them. That is our responsibility as moral agents.

The distinction between facts and decisions about facts gives us, too, an additional reason for rejecting the appeal to any sort of authority. If we say that: 'the psychologist says that I ought not to slipper my children'; or: 'the priest says that I ought not to divorce my wife', it is logically fallacious to conclude that I *therefore* ought to do neither of these things. For it is a *fact* that the psychologist says the first thing and the priest the second. But *we* have to make decisions about facts. And it only follows that we ought not to do these things if we *also* decide that we ought always to do what the psychologist or the priest tell us we should do. Now, if we accept either of these authorities without question we are truly accepting an authority. But it is often the case that these so-called authorities disagree. Which then shall we accept? If we put forward *reasons* for accepting one rather than the other, then we are not accepting either as our final authority. The decision is ours. But it is the sort of decision that saves us from making a lot of other decisions for ourselves. It is a sort of reasoned surrender to authority like that of the man who joins a party and promises always to toe the party line. Whether or not accepting such a provisional authority is consistent with our moral responsibility depends on whether we are prepared to admit that, on occasion, this provisional kind of authority may be wrong, and may have to be rejected.

Now some scientists might readily admit the logic of the matter as we have so far exhibited it; but they might say that a certain branch of modern science – psycho-analysis – has shown the argument advanced to be largely irrelevant. For psycho-analysis has revealed that we can never really get rid of the father. We take him into ourselves when we develop a 'super-ego' around about the age of four and what we call our conscience is, in the main, his forbidding voice which dictates our standards. We have, as it were, got rid of the patriarch in society but have set him up in our own minds.

In meeting this very subtle objection, it is first necessary to point out the ambiguity of the term 'conscience'. It can be used in the context of what we have called customary morality, or doing the done thing. And no doubt the Freudian theory can take very good care of this sort of behaviour. But 'conscience' can also be used to refer to rational reflection on principles. Bishop Butler, for instance, defined 'conscience' as 'a principle of reflection in men, by which they distinguish between, approve and disapprove their own actions'. My account of morality presupposes the use of conscience in this second sense and it is arguable that the Freudian theory has little relevance to it. This contention has support in the theory of the Swiss psychologist, Jean Piaget. For he maintains that children pass through stages in their attitude to rules, whether these are rules of games like marbles, or the rules which regulate society like those against theft and injury to others. At first, the rules seem to them to be externally imposed, emanating from the unquestionable authority of parents and teachers. Of course, they may not keep to the rules; they may cheat or follow their own inclinations. But they do not question the validity of rules. This is the stage of the formation of the Freudian super-ego. It is only later when they emerge into the gang stage that they begin to see that both sorts of rules depend on mutual consent and can be altered if they so decide. They see the *point* of rules and develop quite a different attitude to them. They do not altogether shed their early attitude to rules; in all of us, in varying degrees, our father's voice lives on. But a measure of autonomy is superimposed on this precipitate of parental prohibitions.

Piaget's distinction between the transcendental and autonomous stages of the child's development is as a matter of fact a paradigm of our social development. We have gradually emerged from the closed, traditional, patriarchal sort of society when our lives were governed almost entirely by external unquestionable authorities. Science and morality are two of the most important manifestations of this stage. And they are connected not because the scientist is a new authority to replace the old ones, but because they are both *anti*-authoritarian in character. This is perhaps rather a negative characterization of their relationship. But a further elucidation of what it implies suggests a more positive connection.

Both science and morality, it has been argued, involve being reasonable or the use of reason. This does *not* mean the switching on of some sort of mental gadget which would enable us to split the atom, solve a crossword puzzle, or plan a murder. Extremely unreasonable people can do all these things. It means the determination to follow reasons and to disregard irrelevant considerations, or acting in accordance with certain procedures which are essential to discovering the truth. The rejection of the appeal to authority is the negative facet of the positive demand for the truth. This presupposes some kind of impartiality. Just because *I* say this or *you* say that, it need not be right. The use of reason demands that differences or distinctions should only be made when there are *grounds* for making them. Listening to the other fellow and disregarding irrelevant considerations like the tone of his voice or colour of his eyes, is essential to science or any other form of rational discussion. For why should *these* be grounds for listening or not listening to what he says? And reasonableness, in this general sense, is also essential to morality. For, in morality, we are dealing with practical rather than with theoretical reason; we are dealing with clashes of interests, needs, and claims rather than with clashes of theories as in science. But morality makes a similar requirement of us – that we should consider the proposals under dispute with impartiality. We must not be swayed by considerations which are irrelevant to the issue – as, for example, people's height or physical attractiveness in deciding whether or not they should pay their debts. The immoral person is the one who says what is right for himself need not be right for somebody else. He treats himself as a *privileged* person in the sense that he would not be prepared to accept the justification which he gives for himself acting in a certain way as valid for anyone else. His defence, in effect, is that it is all right for me simply because I am I. Number one must always come first. This is the plea of privilege and partiality, whereas the moral standpoint is that the claims of all who are involved should be assessed in terms of considerations that are relevant to the proposal put forward. When we try to pass on morality to children we say to them: 'How would it be if somebody else did this to you?', or 'How would it be if we all acted like this?' This is not only different from the appeal to privilege; it is also radically different from the authoritarian demand of: 'Don't do this because I say so' – which is, in effect, hindering them from being moral.

This impartiality in science and morality finds its more positive expression in what we call respect for the other fellow. To be partial is to disregard the theories or claims of another person for irrelevant reasons. It also often means just *using* him to advance our own claims. These principles of impartiality and respect for persons can be seen at work in other institutions of our more brotherly sort of society. Equality before the law, for instance, requires that if a person falls into a particular legal category – for example, that of landlord or tenant – he shall not be deprived of what is due to him as a landlord or tenant because of irrelevant considerations such as his religion, height, or social upbringing. Verdicts must be returned in accordance with the evidence and not in accordance with the likes and dislikes of the judge and jury. The defendant and prosecution are allowed full facilities for stating their case so that a *reasonable* decision can be arrived at. Similarly in Parliament, the Prime Minister cannot go down to the House and say: 'I am a great authority; listen to me and do what I say.' He has to give reasons for his policy. The pity is that so much political argument degenerates into abuse of the other side rather than being conducted in a reasonable manner.

Reasonableness, then, which involves impartiality, is the basis of science and morality and is at work in the legal and political institutions of our society. Is this all that can be said about the positive connection between science and morality? Not quite; for there is another very important aspect of the matter.

It is often said that our trouble today is that science has advanced, but our morality has not kept pace with our cleverness. We have developed understanding of the atom, of bacteria, and propaganda; but we are still wicked enough to use these discoveries to destroy each other and warp the minds and bodies of those who stand in the way of our personal, party or national interests. Science, we say, is too much the tool of those who put the pursuit of power and privilege before morality. And, no doubt, there is quite a lot in this thesis. It certainly serves to spotlight the point that I have stressed before – that *we* have to decide what is to be done about discoveries of fact. But the thesis is only partly true; for just as good a case can be made for saying that the reverse is also true – that we are far more moral than we were, but that we have not proved clever enough to keep up with it. This more unusual and less obvious thesis I will now elaborate.

Under the old patriarchal system men regarded codes of conduct and social institutions as imposed on them by some unquestionable external authority. Like Piaget's children in their early years, they never doubted the *validity* of rules. They were handed down by tradition and were felt to be as much part of the universal order of things as the regularities of the seasons and tides. Every man had a place in society like the fish in the sea and the birds in the air. This social order seemed unalterable. Men therefore did not feel much responsibility for social practices and institutions which stunted the lives of so many. It is only with the rise of the fatherless society that men have come to realize that social practices depend on us and that we are responsible for our institutions. Age-old traditions have been challenged, and, when looked at with some measure of impartiality, have been seen to favour the few at the expense of the many. Some of them were based on privilege and irrelevant considerations like those of birth. After all, why should a child be condemned to work in a mine at the age of nine years old, just because of an accident of birth? Or why should not the civil service be open to all, irrespective of their social upbringing?

This dawning realization of the alterability of institutions and of the unfairness of so many age-old traditions has brought with it a new sense of responsibility together with a great zeal for reform. Reforms of all kinds – political, social, medical and educational – have swept the country during the past hundred years. But our moral zeal has, in some ways, proved too much for our cleverness. For in human affairs well-meaning reforms have often unintended consequences which the reformers neither wished for, nor anticipated. For instance, sex equality seems a thoroughly desirable and moral objective; a great deal has been achieved towards bringing it about in the past fifty years. Yet quite recently the secretary of the Marriage Guidance Council claimed that it is the biggest cause of divorce. 'It is the new equality of women with men,' he said, 'that really has shaken the stability of marriage and family life.' Now, this assertion does not entail that we should stop the movement for the equality of the sexes. It merely illustrates the thesis that a much-needed reform has brought in its train a lot of unintended consequences that its initiators were not clever enough to foresee.

This is where the scientist – especially the social scientist and psychologist – may be able to come to the rescue of our morality. For he tries to establish generalizations about the unintended consequences of our actions. Durkheim, for instance, suggested that if we improve the standard of education in a community, we also tend to increase the suicide rate. Now if this were true, it would be a very useful thing for us to know. What we did about it, of course, would still be up to us. But we would not be quite so impetuous in trying to improve things all at once. We would be more in the position of the doctor who wished to introduce sweeping medical improvements in an African territory and who was asked by the administrator: 'But tell me, how are you going to feed all the people you keep alive? We can't grow enough to support them and we can't afford any more imports.' The scientist in such cases does not tell us what we ought to do. But he does help us to make a more clear-headed and responsible decision for ourselves.

Morality can too often take the form of indignation and moralizing. This never gets us very far. It is more important to moralize less and *do* more about clearing up the mess. But this we cannot do unless we understand why there is a mess. And in this the scientist again can help us. We are worried, for instance, about the amount of juvenile delinquency in our midst. If the psychologist tells us that its main cause is lack of maternal care in the early years, then we know the sort of thing to do in order to improve things. The scientist may also be able to tell us that certain methods of clearing up the mess may lead to a worse one which we do not intend.

There is a sense in which human progress has been the substitution of one form of misery for another. We have got rid of most of the injustices and sources of misery of the patriarchal society. But the methods we have adopted have brought in their train miseries of a different kind. Loneliness and the feeling that we do not belong anywhere, for instance, were not social problems in the Middle Ages as they are today. Yet these miseries are in part the product of the centralization of authority which was necessary to remove many of the injustices of the past. In getting rid of old forms of misery we have often opened up new forms, and even new possibilities of misery.

Yet is it not better to be Socrates dissatisfied than a pig satisfied? To be able to love another person is also to expose oneself to depths of misery that a man who can never love can never dream of. But would we therefore give up our capacity for love? Men once suffered in this country because there was little freedom of thought. But freedom of thought, though exhilarating, can also make us very unhappy. Would we then give it up? A certain degree of discontent is the penalty we pay for evolving from the apes. But much of it could be averted with a little informed foresight. It is possible that science – especially the sciences of man – may gradually provide this sort of foresight. In time we may well become wiser to the unintended consequences of our well-meaning reforms and may thus save ourselves from too ham-handed applications of our moral code.

In this partnership between science and morality the scientist's role is not that of an authority. Indeed his advice serves to increase the range of our responsibility rather than to relieve us of it. For if the scientist can tell us what the causes of juvenile delinquency are, he can also tell us how people can be conditioned so as to behave like men in 1984. Responsibility implies that we know what we are doing. Thus the more we know the probable effects of our ways of dealing with children, the greater is our responsibility in relation to them. The scientist, who has so often looked like a new authority on whose shoulders we could cast our responsibilities, has turned out instead to have increased their range. Our danger is that, having killed the father, we may feel over-burdened by our responsibilities and set up the son in his place.

DISCUSSION POINTS

1   Do you agree with the view that today ability counts for more than birth?

2   'The decline of religion in the West is linked with the rise of modern science.' Discuss.

3   Discuss the view that true science is anti-authoritarian.

4   Is talk of a 'new morality' simply an excuse for moral anarchy or are there good reasons why old rules might no longer apply in new situations?

5   '*Conscience* is really the fear of punishment.' Do you agree?

6   'You can never eliminate privilege; it is present in all societies.' Do you agree?

7   'It is waste of time discussing what ought to be. It is more realistic to face the fact that men are what they are – prisoners of their own nature – and to forget morality altogether.' What do you think?

8   'Reasoning with a child is a waste of time; he only understands a good beating.' Consider this view.

9   What do you think of the argument that man's morality has outstripped his cleverness?

10   Do you agree that it is better to be a Socrates dissatisfied rather than a pig satisfied?

PROJECTS

1   Try to find out something about the way parents from different social classes bring up their children and how different moral attitudes seem to result.

2   Observe any group of boys playing (marbles, soccer, etc.). Suggest to them that they might change the rules. Note their reactions.

READING

Patterns of Infant Care, John and Elizabeth Newson (Penguin, 1965). A study of child-rearing practices in Nottingham.

Introduction to Moral Education, J. Wilson, N. Williams and B. Sugarman (Penguin, 1967). Philosophical, psychological and sociological essays on moral education in an increasingly non-religious age.

The Moral Judgement of the Child, J. Piaget (Routledge, 1932). A famous Swiss psychologist studies how the child develops from dependence on his parents to independence in making moral decisions.

Samples From English Culture, J. Klein (Routledge, 1965). A comprehensive survey of studies into English cultural background, with special emphasis on moral upbringing.

George Bernard Shaw
Is democracy a myth?

from the Preface to *The Apple Cart*, Constable, 1930

What is the best form of government for ensuring the widest freedom for the greatest number of people in a society? Many people would say that the answer was democracy. Winston Churchill, for example, once remarked that the worst form of government was democracy – except for all the others. However, in the 1920s and 1930s democracy in Europe was under heavy fire. It was blamed by many for the economic depression and widespread unemployment of that time. In Britain the Fascist movement led by Sir Oswald Mosely, and the Communists inspired by the enormous economic advances of the Soviet Union, worked actively to undermine the democratic system. George Bernard Shaw, in the following passage taken from his Preface to *The Apple Cart*, written in 1930, casts an ironic eye at democracy and in so doing brings out some of its strengths and weaknesses.

On the subject of democracy generally I have nothing to say that can take the problem farther than I have already carried it in my 'Intelligent Woman's Guide to Socialism and Capitalism'. We have to solve two inseparable main problems: the economic problem of how to produce and distribute our subsistence, and the political problem of how to select our rulers and prevent them from abusing their authority in their own interests or those of their class or religion. Our solution of the economic problem is the capitalist system, which achieves miracles in production, but fails so ludicrously and disastrously to distribute its products rationally, or to produce in the order of social need, that it is always complaining of being paralysed by its 'overproduction' of things of which millions of us stand in desperate want. Our solution of the political problem is votes for everybody and every authority elected by vote, an expedient originally devised to prevent rulers from tyrannizing by the very effectual method of preventing them from doing anything, and thus leaving everything to irresponsible private enterprise. But as private enterprise will do nothing that is not profitable to its little self, and the very existence of civilization now depends on the swift and un-hampered public execution of enterprises that supersede private enter-prise and are not merely profitable but vitally necessary to the whole community, this purely inhibitive check on tyranny has become a stranglehold on genuine democracy. Its painfully evolved machinery of parliament and Party System and Cabinet is so effective in obstruction that we take thirty years by constitutional methods to do thirty minutes work, and shall presently be forced to clear up thirty years arrears in thirty minutes by unconstitutional ones unless we pass a reform bill that will make a complete revolution in our political machinery and procedure. When we see parliaments like ours kicked into the gutter by dictators, both in kingdoms and republics, it is foolish to wait until the dictator dies or collapses, and then do nothing but pick the poor old things up and try to scrape the mud off them : the only sane course is to take the step by which the dictatorship could have been anticipated and averted, and construct a political system for rapid positive work instead of slow nugatory work, made to fit into the twentieth century instead of into the sixteenth.

Until we face this task and accomplish it we shall not be able to produce electorates capable of doing anything by their votes except pave the way to their own destruction. An election at present, considered as a means of selecting the best qualified rulers, is so absurd that if the last dozen parliaments had consisted of the candidates who were at the foot of the poll instead of those who were at the head of it there is no reason to suppose that we should have been a step more or less advanced than we are today. In neither case would the electorate have had any real choice of representatives. If it had, we might have had to struggle with parliaments of Titus Oateses and Lord George Gordons dominating a few generals and artists, with cabinets made up of the sort of orator who is said to carry away his hearers by his eloquence because, having first ascertained by a few cautious feelers what they are ready to applaud, he gives it to them a dozen times over in an overwhelming crescendo, and is in effect carried away by them. As it is, the voters have no real choice of candidates: they have to take what they can get and make the best of it according to their lights, which is often the worst of it by the light of heaven. By chance rather than by judgement they find themselves represented in parliament by a fortunate proportion of reasonably honest and public spirited persons who happen to be also successful public speakers. The rest are in parliament because they can afford it and have a fancy for it or an interest in it.

Last October (1929) I was asked to address the enormous audience created by the new invention of wireless broadcast on a range of political and cultural topics introduced by a previous speaker under the general heading of 'Points of View'. Among the topics was democracy, presented, as usual, in a completely abstract guise as an infinitely beneficent principle in which we must trust though it slay us. I was determined that this time votes for everybody and every authority elected by vote should not escape by wearing its imposing mask. I delivered myself as follows:

Your Majesties, your Royal Highnesses, your Excellencies, your Graces and Reverences, my Lords, Ladies and Gentlemen, fellow-citizens of all degrees: I am going to talk to you about democracy objectively: that is, as it exists and as we must all reckon with it equally, no matter what our points of view may be. Suppose I were to talk to you not about democracy, but about the sea, which is in some respects rather like democracy? We all have our own views on the sea. Some of us hate it and are never well when we are at it or on it. Others love it, and are never so happy as when they are in it or on it or looking at it. Some of us regard it as Britain's natural realm and surest bulwark: others want a channel tunnel. But certain facts about the sea are quite independent of our feelings towards it. If I take it for granted that the sea exists, none of you will contradict me. If I say that the sea is sometimes furiously violent and always uncertain, and that those who are most familiar with it trust it least, you will not immediately shriek out that I do not believe in the sea; that I am an enemy of the sea; that I want to abolish the sea; that I am going to make bathing illegal; that I am out to ruin our carrying trade and lay waste all our seaside resorts and scrap the British Navy. If I tell you that you cannot breathe in the sea, you will not take that as a personal insult and ask me indignantly if I consider you inferior to a fish. Well, you must please be equally sensible when I tell you some hard facts about democracy. When I tell you that it is sometimes furiously violent and always dangerous and treacherous, and that those who are familiar with it as practical statesmen trust it least, you must not at once denounce me as a paid agent of Benito Mussolini, or declare that I have become a Tory die-hard in my old age, and accuse me of wanting to take away your votes and make an end of Parliament, and the franchise, and free speech, and public meeting, and trial by jury. Still less must you rise in your places and give me three rousing cheers as a champion of medieval monarchy and feudalism. I am quite innocent of any such extravagances. All I mean is that whether we are Democrats or Tories, Catholics or Protestants, Communists or Fascists, we are all face to face with a certain force in the world called democracy; and we must understand the nature of that force whether we want to fight it or to forward it. Our business is not to deny the perils of democracy, but to provide against them as far as we can, and then consider whether the risks we cannot provide against are worth taking.

Democracy, as you know it, is seldom more than a long word beginning with a capital letter, which we accept reverently or disparage contemptuously without asking any questions. Now we should never accept anything reverently until we have asked it a great many very searching questions, the first two being What are you? and Where do you live? When I put these questions to democracy the answer I get is 'My name is Demos; and I live in the British Empire, the United States of America, and wherever the love of liberty burns in the heart of man. You, my friend Shaw, are a unit of democracy: your name is also Demos: you are a citizen of a great democratic community: you are a potential constituent of the Parliament of Man, the Federation of the World.' At this I usually burst into loud cheers, which do credit to my enthusiastic nature. Tonight, however, I shall do nothing of the sort: I shall say 'Don't talk nonsense. My name is not Demos: it is Bernard Shaw. My address is not the British Empire, nor the United States of America, nor wherever the love of liberty burns in the heart of man: it is at such and such a number in such and such a street in London; and it will be time enough to discuss my seat in the Parliament of Man when that celebrated institution comes into existence. I don't believe your name is Demos: nobody's name is Demos; and all I can make of your address is that you have no address, and are just a tramp – if indeed you exist at all.'

You will notice that I am too polite to call Demos a windbag or a hot air merchant; but I am going to ask you to begin our study of democracy by considering it first as a big balloon, filled with gas or hot air, and sent up so that you shall be kept looking up at the sky whilst other people are picking your pockets. When the balloon comes down to earth every five years or so you are invited to get into the basket if you can throw out one of the people who are sitting tightly in it; but as you can afford neither the time nor the money, and there are forty millions of you and hardly room for six hundred in the basket, the balloon goes up again with much the same lot in it and leaves you where you were before. I think you will admit that the balloon as an image of democracy corresponds to the parliamentary facts.

Now let us examine a more poetic conception of democracy. Abraham Lincoln is represented as standing amid the carnage of the battlefield of Gettysburg, and declaring that all that slaughter of Americans by Americans occurred in order that democracy, defined as government *of* the people *for* the people *by* the people, should not perish from the earth. Let us pick this famous peroration to pieces and see what there really is inside it. (By the way, Lincoln did not really declaim it on the field of Gettysburg; and the American Civil War was not fought in defence of any such principle, but, on the contrary, to enable one half of the United States to force the other half to be governed as they did not wish to be governed. But never mind that. I mentioned it only to remind you that it seems impossible for statesmen to make speeches about democracy, or journalists to report them, without obscuring it in a cloud of humbug.)

Now for the three articles of the definition. Number One: Government *of* the people: that, evidently, is necessary: a human community can no more exist without a government than a human being can exist without a co-ordinated control of its breathing and blood circulation. Number Two: Government *for* the people, is most important. Dean Inge put it perfectly for us when he called democracy a form of society which means equal consideration for all. He added that it is a Christian principle, and that, as a Christian, he believes in it. So do I. That is why I insist on equality of income. Equal consideration for a person with a hundred a year and one with a hundred thousand is impossible. But Number Three: Government *by* the people, is quite a different matter. All the monarchs, all the tyrants, all the dictators, all the die-hard Tories are agreed that we must be governed. Democrats like the Dean and myself are agreed that we must be governed with equal consideration for everybody. But we repudiate Number Three on the ground that the people cannot govern. The thing is a physical impossibility. Every citizen cannot be a ruler any more than every boy can be an engine driver or a pirate king. A nation of prime ministers or dictators is as absurd as an army of field marshals. Government by the people is not and never can be a reality: it is only a cry by which demagogues humbug us into voting for them. If you doubt this – if you ask me 'Why should not the people make their own laws?' I need only ask you 'Why should not the people write their own plays?' They cannot. It is much easier to write a good play than to make a good law. And there are not a hundred men in the world who can write a play good enough to stand daily wear and tear as long as a law must.

Now comes the question, If we cannot govern ourselves, what can we do to save ourselves from being at the mercy of those who *can* govern, and who may quite possibly be thoroughpaced grafters and scoundrels? The primitive answer is that as we are always in a huge majority we can, if rulers oppress us intolerably, burn their houses and tear them to pieces. This is not satisfactory. Decent people never do it until they have quite lost their heads; and when they have lost their heads they are as likely as not to burn the wrong house and tear the wrong man to pieces. When we have what is called a popular movement very few people who take part in it know what it is all about. I once saw a real popular movement in London. People were running excitedly through the streets. Everyone who saw them doing it immediately joined in the rush. They ran simply because everyone else was doing it. It was most impressive to see thousands of people sweeping along at full speed like that. There could be no doubt that it was literally a popular movement. I ascertained afterwards that it was started by a runaway cow. That cow had an important share in my education as a political philosopher; and I can assure you that if you will study crowds, and lost and terrified animals, and things like that, instead of reading books and newspaper articles, you will learn a great deal about politics from them. Most general elections, for instance, are nothing but stampedes. Our last but one was a conspicuous example of this. The cow was a Russian one.

I think we may take it that neither mob violence nor popular movements can be depended on as checks upon the abuse of power by governments. One might suppose that at least they would act as a last resort when an autocrat goes mad and commits outrageous excesses of tyranny and cruelty. But it is a curious fact that they never do. Take two famous cases: those of Nero and Tsar Paul the First of Russia. If Nero had been an ordinary professional fiddler he would probably have been no worse a man than any member of the wireless orchestra. If Paul had been a lieutenant in a line regiment we should never have heard of him. But when these two poor fellows were invested with absolute powers over their fellow-creatures they went mad, and did such appalling things that they had to be killed like mad dogs. Only, it was not the people that rose up and killed them. They were dispatched quite privately by a very select circle of their own bodyguards. For a genuinely democratic execution of unpopular statesmen we must turn to the brothers De Witt, who were torn to pieces by a Dutch mob in the seventeenth century. They were neither tyrants nor autocrats. On the contrary, one of them had been imprisoned and tortured for his resistance to the despotism of William of Orange; and the other had come to meet him as he came out of prison. The mob was on the side of the autocrat. We may take it that the shortest way for a tyrant to get rid of a troublesome champion of liberty is to raise a hue and cry against him as an unpatriotic person, and leave the mob to do the rest after supplying them with a well tipped ringleader. Nowadays this is called direct action by the revolutionary proletariat. Those who put their faith in it soon find that proletariats are never revolutionary, and that their direct action, when it is controlled at all, is usually controlled by police agents.

Democracy, then, cannot be government by the people: it can only be government by consent of the governed. Unfortunately, when democratic statesmen propose to govern us by our own consent, they find that we don't want to be governed at all, and that we regard rates and taxes and rents and death duties as intolerable burdens. What we want to know is how little government we can get along with without being murdered in our beds. That question cannot be answered until we have explained what we mean by getting along. Savages manage to get along. Unruly Arabs and Tartars get along. The only rule in the matter is that the civilized way of getting along is the way of corporate action, not individual action; and corporate action involves more government than individual action.

Thus government, which used to be a comparatively simple affair, today has to manage an enormous development of Socialism and Communism. Our industrial and social life is set in a huge communistic framework of public roadways, streets, bridges, water supplies, power supplies, lighting, tramways, schools, dockyards, and public aids and conveniences, employing a prodigious army of police, inspectors, teachers, and officials of all grades in hundreds of departments. We have found by bitter experience that it is impossible to trust factories, workshops, and mines to private management. Only by stern laws enforced by constant inspection have we stopped the monstrous waste of human life and welfare it cost when it was left uncontrolled by the Government. During the war our attempt to leave the munitioning of the army to private enterprise led us to the verge of defeat and caused an appalling slaughter of our soldiers. When the Government took the work out of private hands and had it done in national factories it was at once successful. The private firms were still allowed to do what little they could; but they had to be taught to do it economically, and to keep their accounts properly, by Government officials. Our big capitalist enterprises now run to the Government for help as a lamb runs to its mother. They cannot even make an extension of the tube railway in London without Government aid. Unassisted private capitalism is breaking down or getting left behind in all directions. If all our Socialism and Communism and the drastic taxation of unearned incomes which finances it were to stop, our private enterprises would drop like shot stags, and we should all be dead in a month. When Mr Baldwin tried to win the last election by declaring that Socialism had been a failure whenever and wherever it had been tried, Socialism went over him like a steam roller and handed his office to a Socialist Prime Minister. Nothing could save us in the war but a great extension of Socialism; and now it is clear enough that only still greater extensions of it can repair the ravages of the war and keep pace with the growing requirements of civilization.

What we have to ask ourselves, then, is not whether we will have Socialism and Communism or not, but whether democracy can keep pace with the developments of both that are being forced on us by the growth of national and international corporate action.

Now corporate action is impossible without a governing body. It may be the central government: it may be a municipal corporation, a county council, a district council, or a parish council. It may be the board of directors of a joint stock company, or of a trust made by combining several joint stock companies. Such boards, elected by the votes of the shareholders, are little states within the State, and very powerful ones, too, some of them. If they have not laws and kings, they have by-laws and chairmen. And you and I, the consumers of their services, are more at the mercy of the boards that organize them than we are at the mercy of parliament. Several active politicians who began as Liberals and are now Socialists have said to me that they were converted by seeing that the nation had to choose, not between governmental control of industry and control by separate private individuals kept in order by their competition for our custom, but between governmental control and control by gigantic trusts wielding great power without responsibility, and having no object but to make as much money out of us as possible. Our Government is at this moment having much more trouble with the private corporations on whom we are dependent for our coals and cotton goods than with France or the United States of America. We are in the hands of our corporate bodies, public or private, for the satisfaction of our everyday needs. Their powers are life and death powers. I need not labour this point: we all know it.

But what we do not all realize is that we are equally dependent on corporate action for the satisfaction of our religious needs. Dean Inge tells us that our general elections have become public auctions at which the contending parties bid against one another for our votes by each promising us a larger share than the other of the plunder of the minority. Now that is perfectly true. The contending parties do not as yet venture to put it exactly in those words; but that is what it comes to. And the Dean's profession obliges him to urge his congregation, which is much wider than that of St Paul's (it extends across the Atlantic), always to vote for the party which pledges itself to go farthest in enabling those of us who have great possessions to sell them and give the price to the poor. But we cannot do this as private persons. It must be done by the Government or not at all. Take my own case. I am not a young man with great possessions; but I am an old man paying enough in income tax and surtax to provide doles for some hundreds of unemployed and old age pensioners. I have not the smallest objection to this: on the contrary, I advocated it strongly for years before I had any income worth taxing. But I could not do it if the Government did not arrange it for me. If the Government ceased taxing my superfluous money and redistributing it among people who have no incomes at all, I could do nothing by myself. What could I do? Can you suggest anything? I could send my war bonds to the Chancellor of the Exchequer and invite him to cancel the part of the National Debt that they represent; and he would undoubtedly thank me in the most courteous official terms for my patriotism. But the poor would not get any of it. The other payers of surtax and income tax and death duties would save the interest they now have to pay on it: that is all. I should only have made the rich richer and myself poorer. I could burn all my share certificates and inform the secretaries of the companies that they might write off that much of their capital indebtedness. The result would be a bigger dividend for the rest of the shareholders, with the poor out in the cold as before. I might sell my war bonds and share certificates for cash, and throw the money into the street to be scrambled for; but it would be snatched up, not by the poorest, but by the best fed and most able-bodied of the scramblers. Besides, if we all tried to sell our bonds and shares – and this is what you have to consider; for Christ's advice was not addressed to me alone but to all who have great possessions – the result would be that their value would fall to nothing, as the Stock Exchange would immediately become a market in which there were all sellers and no buyers. Accordingly, any spare money that the Government leaves me is invested where I can get the highest interest and the best security, as thereby I can make sure that it goes where it is most wanted and gives immediate employment. This is the best I can do without Government interference: indeed any other way of dealing with my spare money would be foolish and demoralizing; but the result is that I become richer and richer, and the poor become relatively poorer and poorer. So you see I cannot even be a Christian except through Government action; and neither can the Dean.

Now let us get down to our problem. We cannot govern ourselves; yet if we entrust the immense powers and revenues which are necessary in an effective modern Government to an absolute monarch or dictator, he goes more or less mad unless he is a quite extraordinary and therefore very seldom obtainable person. Besides, modern government is not a one-man job: it is too big for that. If we resort to a committee or parliament of superior persons, they will set up an oligarchy and abuse their power for their own benefit. Our dilemma is that men in the lump cannot govern themselves; and yet, as William Morris put it, no man is good enough to be another man's master. We need to be governed, and yet to control our governors. But the best governors will not accept any control except that of their own consciences; and, as we who are governed are also apt to abuse any power of control we have, our ignorance, our passions, our private and immediate interests are constantly in conflict with the knowledge, the wisdom, and the public spirit and regard for the future of our best qualified governors.

Still, if we cannot control our governors, can we not at least choose them and change them if they do not suit?

Let me invent a primitive example of democratic choice. It is always best to take imaginary examples: they offend nobody. Imagine then that we are the inhabitants of a village. We have to elect somebody for the office of postman. There are several candidates; but one stands out conspicuously, because he has frequently treated us at the public-house, has subscribed a shilling to our little flower show, has a kind word for the children when he passes, and is a victim of oppression by the squire because his late father was one of our most successful poachers. We elect him triumphantly; and he is duly installed, uniformed, provided with a red bicycle and given a batch of letters to deliver. As his motive in seeking the post has been pure ambition, he has not thought much beforehand about his duties; and it now occurs to him for the first time that he cannot read. So he hires a boy to come round with him and read the addresses. The boy conceals himself in the lane whilst the postman delivers the letters at the house, takes the Christmas boxes, and gets the whole credit of the transaction. In course of time he dies with a high reputation for efficiency in the discharge of his duties; and we elect another equally illiterate successor on similar grounds. But by this time the boy has grown up and become an institution. He presents himself to the new postman as an established and indispensable feature of the postal system, and finally becomes recognized and paid by the village as such.

Here you have the perfect image of a popularly elected Cabinet Minister and the Civil Service department over which he presides. It may work very well; for our postman, though illiterate, may be a very capable fellow; and the boy who reads the addresses for him may be quite incapable of doing anything more. But this does not always happen. Whether it happens or not, the system is not a democratic reality: it is a democratic illusion. The boy, when he has ability enough to take advantage of the situation, is the master of the man. The person elected to do the work is not really doing it: he is a popular humbug who is merely doing what a permanent official tells him to do. That is how it comes about that we are now governed by a Civil Service which has such enormous power that its regulations are taking the place of the laws of England, though some of them are made for the convenience of the officials without the slightest regard to the convenience or even the rights of the public. And how are our Civil Servants selected? Mostly by an educational test which nobody but an expensively-schooled youth can pass, thus making the most powerful and effective part of our government an irresponsible class government.

DISCUSSION POINTS

1   The voters in a General Election have no real choice, says Shaw. They have to take what they can get and make the best of it. Do you agree?

2   There is a great deal of talk these days about the need for more people to 'participate' in government. Shaw says, 'Every citizen cannot be a ruler any more than every boy can be an engine driver or a pirate king. A nation of prime ministers is as absurd as an army of field marshals.' What do you think?

3   Shaw likens popular movements to animal stampedes. Are all such changes of political opinion irrational and hysterical?

4   Do you agree with Shaw that mob violence is no check on governments?

5   'What we want to know,' writes Shaw, 'is how little government we can get along with without being murdered in our beds.' Do you accept this view or do you think that there should be more and stronger government in Britain?

6   What is more dangerous to liberty in a democracy – the abuse of power by governors or the abuse of power to control governors by those who are being governed?

7   Politicians are often attacked for failing to keep promises, and sometimes defend themselves by saying that only when they got into office did they discover what could or could not be done. Is this a reasonable defence or not?

8   Shaw suggests that democracy is an illusion, just a big word we accept without question. Do you agree, and what about 'liberty'? Is that also an impossibility?

PROJECT

Find out as much as you can about one of the following: (a) How a General Election is organized (in particular find out how candidates are chosen and how Ministers and Prime Ministers are elected); (b) How local elections are organized (try to discover how many people actually voted at your last local election compared with those who were entitled to vote; then ask yourself how more people could be encouraged to participate in local affairs); (c) How a new law is introduced (in particular try to find out about the work of pressure groups interested in getting a new law into operation).

READING

Voters, Parties and Leaders, J. Blondel (Penguin, 1963). A study of the social background and attitudes of voters and politicians giving some idea of where power lies in Britain and how it is used.

British Political Parties, R. T. McKenzie (Heinemann, 1955). A book which is regarded as the standard work on the subject of the title.

David Butler has written several accounts of British General Elections. There is for example *The British General Election of 1959* which he wrote with R. Rose (Macmillan, 1960).

Parliament, Sir I. Jennings (CUP, 1957). An account of the workings and procedures of the upper and lower houses of Parliament.

Small-town Politics, A. H. Birch (OUP, 1959). A book whose title speaks for itself.

Pressure Group Politics, J. D. Stewart (OUP, 1958).

Pressure Group, H. H. Wilson (Secker & Warburg, 1961). An account of the successful campaign to institute commercial television in Britain.

Erich Fromm

Alienation under capitalism

from *The Sane Society*, Routledge & Kegan Paul, 1956

The introduction of mass production techniques which are the main feature of a modern industrial society brings many positive benefits. They increase man's capacity to produce wealth and enable many of the damaging effects of poverty to be eliminated. But industrialization may also produce less desirable results – a decline in traditional craftsmanship, an increase in the number of dull routine jobs, and the growth of large-scale organizations in which workers feel increasingly alienated from management. In the following chapter from his book, *The Sane Society*, Erich Fromm, the American psychologist, explores some of the harmful effects he sees modern capitalism to have had on man's personality.

The central issue of the effects of capitalism on personality [is] the phenomenon of alienation.

By alienation is meant a mode of experience in which the person experiences himself as an alien. He has become, one might say, estranged from himself. He does not experience himself as the centre of his world, as the creator of his own acts – but his acts and their consequences have become his masters, whom he obeys, or whom he may even worship. The alienated person is out of touch with himself as he is out of touch with any other person. He, like the others, is experienced as things are experienced; with the senses and with common sense, but at the same time without being related to himself and to the world outside productively.

The older meaning in which 'alienation' was used was to denote an insane person; *aliéné* in French, *alienado* in Spanish are older words for the psychotic, the thoroughly and absolutely alienated person. ('Alienist' in English, is still used for the doctor who cares for the insane.)

In the last century the word 'alienation' was used by Hegel and Marx, referring not to a state of insanity, but to a less drastic form of self-estrangement, which permits the person to act reasonably in practical matters, yet which constitutes one of the most severe socially patterned defects. In Marx's system alienation is called that condition of man where his 'own act becomes to him an alien power, standing over and against him, instead of being ruled by him.'

But while the use of the word 'alienation' in this general sense is a recent one, the concept is a much older one; it is the same to which the prophets of the Old Testament referred as *idolatry*. It will help us to a better understanding of 'alienation' if we begin by considering the meaning of 'idolatry'.

The prophets of monotheism did not denounce heathen religions as idolatrous primarily because they worshipped several gods instead of one. The essential difference between monotheism and polytheism is not of the *number* of gods, but lies in the fact of self-alienation. Man spends his energy, his artistic capacities on building an idol, and then he worships this idol, which is nothing but the result of his own human effort. His life forces have flown into a 'thing', and this thing, having become an idol, is not experienced as a result of his own productive effort, but as something apart from himself, over and against him, which he worships and to which he submits. As the prophet Hosea says (XIV, 8): 'Assur shall not save us; we will not ride upon horses; *neither will we say any more to the work of our hands, you are our gods*; for in thee the fatherless finds love.' Idolatrous man bows down to the work of his own hands. *The idol represents his own life-forces in an alienated form.*

The principle of monotheism, in contrast, is that man is infinite, that there is no partial quality in him which can be hypostatized into the whole. God, in the monotheistic concept, is unrecognizable and in-definable; God is not a 'thing'. If man is created in the likeness of God, he is created as the bearer of infinite qualities. In idolatry man bows down and submits to the projection of one partial quality in himself. He does not experience himself as the centre from which living acts of love and reason radiate. He becomes a thing, his neighbour becomes a thing, just as his gods are things. 'The idols of the heathen are silver and gold, the work of men's hands. They have mouths but they speak not; eyes have they, but they see not; they have ears but they hear not; neither is there any breath in their mouths. They that make them are like them; so is everyone that trusts in them.' (Psalm 135.)

Monotheistic religions themselves have, to a large extent, regressed into idolatry. Man projects his power of love and of reason unto God; he does not feel them any more as his own powers, and then he prays to God to give him back some of what he, man, has projected unto God. In early Protestantism and Calvinism, the required religious attitude is that man *should* feel himself empty and impoverished, and put his trust in the grace of God, that is, into the hope that God may return to him part of his own qualities, which he has put into God.

Every act of submissive worship is an act of alienation and idolatry in this sense. What is frequently called 'love' is often nothing but this idolatrous phenomenon of alienation; only that not God or an idol, but another person is worshipped in this way. The 'loving' person in this type of submissive relationship, projects all his or her love, strength, thought, into the other person, and experiences the loved person as a superior being, finding satisfaction in complete submission and worship. This does not only mean that he fails to experience the loved person as a human being in his or her reality, but that he does not experience *himself* in his full reality, as the bearer of productive human powers. Just as in the case of religious idolatry, he has projected all his richness into the other person, and experiences this richness not any more as something which is his, but as something alien from himself, deposited in somebody else, with which he can get in touch only by submission to, or submergence in, the other person. The same phenomenon exists in the worshipping submission to a political leader, or to the State. The leader and the State actually are what they are by the consent of the governed. But they become idols when the individual projects all his powers into them and worships them, hoping to regain some of his powers by submission and worship.

In Rousseau's theory of the State, as in contemporary totalitarianism, the individual is supposed to abdicate his own rights and to project them unto the State as the only arbiter. In Fascism and Stalinism the absolutely alienated individual worships at the altar of an idol, and it makes little difference by what names this idol is known: State, class, collective, or what else.

We can speak of idolatry or alienation not only in relationship to other people, but also in relationship to oneself, when the person is subject to irrational passions. The person who is mainly motivated by his lust for power, does not experience himself any more in the richness and limitlessness of a human being, but he becomes a slave to one partial striving in him, which is projected into external aims, by which he is 'possessed'. The person who is given to the exclusive pursuit of his passion for money is possessed by his striving for it; money is the idol which he worships as the projection of one isolated power in himself, his greed for it. In this sense, the neurotic person is an alienated person. His actions are not his own; while he is under the illusion of doing what *he* wants, he is driven by forces which are separated from his self, which work behind his back; he is a stranger to himself, just as his fellow man is a stranger to him. He experiences the other and himself not as what they really are, but distorted by the unconscious forces which operate in them. The insane person is the *absolutely alienated* person; he has completely lost himself as the centre of his own experience; he has lost the sense of self.

What is common to all these phenomena – the worship of idols, the idolatrous worship of God, the idolatrous love for a person, the worship of a political leader or the State, and the idolatrous worship of the externalizations of irrational passions – is the process of alienation. It is the fact that *man does not experience himself as the active bearer of his own powers and richness, but as an impoverished 'thing', dependent on powers outside of himself, unto whom he has projected his living substance.*

As the reference to idolatry indicates, alienation is by no means a modern phenomenon. Suffice it to say that it seems alienation differs from culture to culture, both in the specific spheres which are alienated, and in the thoroughness and completeness of the process.

Alienation as we find it in modern society is almost total; it pervades the relationship of man to his work, to the things he consumes, to the State, to his fellow man, and to himself. Man has created a world of man-made things as it never existed before. He has constructed a complicated social machine to administer the technical machine he built. Yet this whole creation of his stands over and above him. He does not feel himself as a creator and centre, but as the servant of a Golem, which his hands have built. The more powerful and gigantic the forces are which he unleashes, the more powerless he feels himself as a human being. He confronts himself with his own forces embodied in things he has created, alienated from himself. He is owned by his own creation, and has lost ownership of himself. He has built a golden calf, and says 'these are your gods who have brought you out of Egypt'.

What happens to the *worker*? To put it in the words of a thoughtful and thorough observer of the industrial scene: 'In industry the person becomes an economic atom that dances to the tune of atomistic management. Your place is just here, you will sit in this fashion, your arms will move x inches in a course of y radius and the time of movement will be ·ooo minutes.

'Work is becoming more repetitive and thoughtless as the planners, the micromotionists, and the scientific managers further strip the worker of his right to think and move freely. Life is being denied; need to control, creativeness, curiosity, and independent thought are being baulked, and the result, the inevitable result, is flight or fight on the part of the worker, apathy or destructiveness, psychic regression.' [J. J. Gillespie.]

The role of the *manager* is also one of alienation. It is true, he manages the whole and not a part, but he too is alienated from his product as something concrete and useful. His aim is to employ profitably the capital invested by others, although in comparison with the older type of owner-manager, modern management is much less interested in the amount of profit to be paid out as dividend to the stockholder than it is in the efficient operation and expansion of the enterprise. Characteristically, within management those in charge of labour relations and of sales – that is, of human manipulation – gain, relatively speaking, an increasing importance in comparison with those in charge of the technical aspects of production.

The manager, like the worker, like everybody, deals with impersonal giants: with the giant competitive enterprise; with the giant national and world market; with the giant consumer, who has to be coaxed and manipulated; with the giant unions, and the giant government. All these giants have their own lives, as it were. They determine the activity of the manager and they direct the activity of the worker and clerk.

The problem of the manager opens up one of the most significant phenomena in an alienated culture, that of *bureaucratization*. Both big business and government administrations are conducted by a bureaucracy. Bureaucrats are specialists in the administration of things *and of men*. Due to the bigness of the apparatus to be administered, and the resulting abstractification, the bureaucrats' relationship to the people is one of complete alienation. They, the people to be administered, are objects whom the bureaucrats consider neither with love nor with hate, but completely impersonally; the manager-bureaucrat must not feel, as far as his professional activity is concerned; he must manipulate people as though they were figures, or things. Since the vastness of the organization and the extreme division of labour prevents any single individual from seeing the whole, since there is no organic, spontaneous co-operation between the various individuals or groups within the industry, the managing bureaucrats are necessary; without them the enterprise would collapse in a short time, since nobody would know the secret which makes it function. Bureaucrats are as indispensable as the tons of paper consumed under their leadership. Just because everybody senses, with a feeling of powerlessness, the vital role of the bureaucrats, they are given an almost godlike respect. If it were not for the bureaucrats, people feel, everything would go to pieces, and we would starve. Whereas, in the medieval world, the leaders were considered representatives of a god-intended order, in modern capitalism the role of the bureaucrat is hardly less sacred – since he is necessary for the survival of the whole.

Marx gave a profound definition of the bureaucrat saying: 'The bureaucrat relates himself to the world as a *mere object* of his activity.' It is interesting to note that the spirit of bureaucracy has entered not only business and government administration, but also trade unions and the great democratic socialist parties in England, Germany and France. In Russia, too, the bureaucratic managers and their alienated spirit have conquered the country. Russia could perhaps exist without terror – if certain conditions were given – but it could not exist without the system of total bureaucratization – that is, alienation.

What is the attitude of the *owner* of the enterprise, the capitalist? The small businessman seems to be in the same position as his predecessor a hundred years ago. He owns and directs his small enterprise, he is in touch with the whole commercial or industrial activity, and in personal contact with his employees and workers. But living in an alienated world in all other economic and social aspects, and furthermore being more under the constant pressure of bigger competitors, he is by no means as free as his grandfather was in the same business.

But what matters more and more in contemporary economy is big business, the large corporation. And the attitude of the 'owner' of the big corporation to 'his' property is one of almost complete alienation. His ownership consists in a piece of paper, representing a certain fluctuating amount of money; he has no responsibility for the enterprise and no concrete relationship to it in any way.

The process of *consumption* is as alienated as the process of production. In the first place, we acquire things with money; we are accustomed to this and take it for granted. But actually, this is a most peculiar way of acquiring things. Money represents labour and effort in an abstract form; not necessarily *my* labour and *my* effort, since I can have acquired it by inheritance, by fraud, by luck, or any number of ways. But even if I have acquired it by *my* effort (forgetting for the moment that *my* effort might not have brought me the money were it not for the fact that I employed men), I have acquired it in a specific way, by a specific kind of effort, corresponding to my skills and capacities, while, in spending, the money is transformed into an abstract form of labour and can be exchanged against anything else. Provided I am in the possession of money, no effort or interest of mine is necessary to acquire something. If I have the money, I can acquire an exquisite painting, even though I may not have any appreciation for art; I can buy the best phonograph, even though I have no musical taste; I can buy a library, although I use it only for the purpose of ostentation. I can buy an education, even though I have no use of it except as an additional social asset. I can even destroy the painting or the books I bought, and aside from a loss of money, I suffer no damage. Mere possession of money gives me the right to acquire and to do with my acquisition whatever I like. The *human* way of acquiring would be to make an effort qualitatively commensurate with what I acquire. The acquisition of bread and clothing would depend on no other premise than that of being alive; the acquisition of books and paintings, on my effort to understand them and my ability to use them. How this principle could be applied practically is not the point to be discussed here. What matters is that the way we acquire things is separated from the way in which we use them.

The alienating function of money in the process of acquisition and consumption has been beautifully described by Marx in the following words: 'Money . . . transforms the real human and natural powers into merely abstract ideas, and hence imperfections, and on the other hand it transforms the real imperfections and imaginings, the powers which only exist in the imagination of the individual into real powers. . . . It transforms loyalty into vice, vice into virtue, the slave into the master, the master into the slave, ignorance into reason, and reason into ignorance. . . . He who can buy valour is valiant although he be cowardly. . . . Assume *man* as *man*, and his relation to the world as a human one, and you can exchange love only for love, confidence for confidence, etc. If you wish to enjoy art, you must be an artistically trained person; if you wish to have influence on other people, you must be a person who has a really stimulating and furthering influence on other people. Every one of your relationships to man and to nature must be a definite expression of our *real, individual* life corresponding to the object of your will. If you love without calling forth love, that is, if your love as such does not produce love, if by means of an *expression of life* as a loving person you do not make of yourself a *loved person*, then your love is impotent, a misfortune.'

But beyond the method of acquisition, how do we use things, once we have acquired them? With regard to many things, there is not even the pretence of use. We acquire them to *have* them. We are satisfied with useless possession. The expensive dining set or crystal vase which we never use for fear they might break, the mansion with many unused rooms, the unnecessary cars and servants, like the ugly bric-a-brac of the lower-middle-class family, are so many examples of pleasure in possession instead of in use. However, this satisfaction in possessing per se was more prominent in the nineteenth century; today most of the satisfaction is derived from possession of things-to-be-used rather than of things-to-be-kept. This does not alter the fact, however, that even in the pleasure of things-to-be-used the satisfaction of prestige is a paramount factor. The car, the refrigerator, the television set are for real, but also for conspicuous use. They confer status on the owner.

How do we use the things we acquire? Let us begin with food and drink. We eat a bread which is tasteless and not nourishing because it appeals to our fantasy of wealth and distinction – being so white and 'fresh'. Actually, we 'eat' a fantasy and have lost contact with the real thing we eat. Our palate, our body, are excluded from an act of consumption which primarily concerns them. We drink labels. With a bottle of Coca-Cola we drink the picture of the pretty boy and girl who drink it in the advertisement, we drink the slogan of 'the pause that refreshes', we drink the great American habit; least of all do we drink with our palate. All this is even worse when it comes to the consumption of things whose whole reality is mainly the fiction the advertising campaign has created, like the 'healthy' soap or dental paste.

I could go on giving examples ad infinitum. But it is unnecessary to belabour the point, since everybody can think of as many illustrations as I could give. I only want to stress the principle involved: the act of consumption should be a concrete human act, in which our senses, bodily needs, our aesthetic taste – that is to say, in which *we* as concrete, sensing, feeling, judging human beings – are involved; the act of consumption should be a meaningful, human, productive experience. In our culture, there is little of that. Consuming is essentially the satisfaction of artificially stimulated fantasies, a fantasy performance alienated from our concrete, real selves.

There is another aspect of alienation from the things we consume which needs to be mentioned. We are surrounded by things of whose nature and origin we know nothing. The telephone, radio, phonograph, and all other complicated machines are almost as mysterious to us as they would be to a man from a primitive culture; we know how to use them, that is, we know which button to turn, but we do not know on what principle they function, except in the vaguest terms of something we once learned at school. And things which do not rest upon difficult scientific principles are almost equally alien to us. We do not know how bread is made, how cloth is woven, how a table is manufactured, how glass is made. We consume, as we produce, without any concrete relatedness to the objects with which we deal; we live in a world of things, and our only connection with them is that we know how to manipulate or to consume them.

Our way of consumption necessarily results in the fact that we are never satisfied, since it is not our real concrete person which consumes a real and concrete thing. We thus develop an ever-increasing need for more things, for more consumption. It is true that as long as the living standard of the population is below a dignified level of subsistence, there is a natural need for more consumption. It is also true that there is a legitimate need for more consumption as man develops culturally and has more refined needs for better food, objects of artistic pleasure, books, etc. But our craving for consumption has lost all connection with the real needs of man. Originally, the idea of consuming more and better things was meant to give man a happier, more satisfied life. Consumption was a means to an end, that of happiness. It now has become an aim in itself. The constant increase of needs forces us to an ever-increasing effort, it makes us dependent on these needs and on the people and institutions by whose help we attain them. 'Each person speculates to create a new need in the other person, in order to force him into a new dependency, to a new form of pleasure, hence to his economic ruin. . . . With a multitude of commodities grows the realm of alien things which enslave man.' [Marx.]

Man today is fascinated by the possibility of buying more, better, and especially, new things. He is consumption-hungry. The act of buying and consuming has become a compulsive, irrational aim, because it is an end in itself, with little relation to the use of, or pleasure in the things bought and consumed. To buy the latest gadget, the latest model of anything that is on the market, is the dream of everybody, in comparison to which the real pleasure in use is quite secondary. Modern man, if he dared to be articulate about his concept of heaven, would describe a vision which would look like the biggest department store in the world, showing new things and gadgets, and himself having plenty of money with which to buy them. He would wander around open-mouthed in this heaven of gadgets and commodities, provided only that there were ever more and new things to buy, and perhaps that his neighbours were just a little less privileged than he.

Significantly enough, one of the older traits of middle-class society, the attachment to possessions and property, has undergone a profound change. In the older attitude, a certain sense of loving possession existed between a man and his property. It grew on him. He was proud of it. He took good care of it, and it was painful when eventually he had to part from it because it could not be used any more. There is very little left of this sense of property today. One loves the newness of the thing bought, and is ready to betray it when something newer has appeared.

Expressing the same change in characterological terms, I can refer to what has been stated above with regard to the *hoarding* orientation as dominant in the picture of the nineteenth century. In the middle of the twentieth century the hoarding orientation has given way to the *receptive* orientation, in which the aim is to receive, to 'drink in', to have something new all the time, to live with a continuously open mouth, as it were. This receptive orientation is blended with the marketing orientation, while in the nineteenth century the hoarding was blended with the exploitative orientation.

The alienated attitude towards consumption not only exists in our acquisition and consumption of commodities, but it determines far beyond this the employment of leisure time. What are we to expect? If a man works without genuine relatedness to what he is doing, if he buys and consumes commodities in an abstractified and alienated way, how can he make use of his leisure time in an active and meaningful way? He always remains the passive and alienated consumer. He 'consumes' ball games, moving pictures, newspapers and magazines, books, lectures, natural scenery, social gatherings, in the same alienated and abstractified way in which he consumes the commodities he has bought. He does not participate actively, he wants to 'take in' all there is to be had, and to have as much as possible of pleasure, culture and what not. Actually, he is not free to enjoy 'his' leisure; his leisure time consumption is determined by industry, as are the commodities he buys; his taste is manipulated, he wants to see and to hear what he is conditioned to want to see and to hear; entertainment is an industry like any other, the customer is made to buy fun as he is made to buy dresses and shoes. The value of the fun is determined by its success on the market, not by anything which could be measured in human terms.

In any productive and spontaneous activity, something happens within myself while I am reading, looking at scenery, talking to friends, etcetera. I am not the same after the experience as I was before. In the alienated form of pleasure nothing happens within me; I have consumed this or that; nothing is changed within myself, and all that is left are memories of what I have done.

Man is not only alienated from the work he does, and the things and pleasures he consumes, but also from the *social forces* which determine our society and the life of everybody living in it.

Our actual helplessness before the forces which govern us appears more drastically in those social catastrophes which, even though they are denounced as regrettable accidents each time, so far have never failed to happen: economic depressions and wars. These social phenomena appear as if they were natural catastrophes, rather than what they really are, occurrences made by man, but without intention and awareness.

This anonymity of the social forces is inherent in the structure of the capitalist mode of production.

In contrast to most other societies in which social laws are explicit and fixed on the basis of political power or tradition – capitalism does not have such explicit laws. It is based on the principle that if only everybody strives for himself on the market, the common good will come of it; order and not anarchy will be the result. There are, of course, economic laws which govern the market, but these laws operate behind the back of the acting individual, who is concerned only with his private interests. You try to guess these laws of the market as a Calvinist in Geneva tried to guess whether God had predestined him for salvation or not. But the laws of the market, like God's will, are beyond the reach of your will and influence.

To a large extent the development of capitalism has proven that this principle works; and it is indeed a miracle that the antagonistic co-operation of self-contained economic entities should result in a blossoming and ever-expanding society. It is true that the capitalistic mode of production is conducive to political freedom, while any centrally planned social order is in danger of leading to political regimentation and eventually to dictatorship. While this is not the place to discuss the question of whether there are other alternatives than the choice between 'free enterprise' and political regimentation, it needs to be said in this context that the very fact that we are governed by laws which we do not control, and do not even want to control, is one of the most outstanding manifestations of alienation. *We* are the producers of our economic and social arrangements, and at the same time we decline responsibility, intentionally and enthusiastically, and await hopefully or anxiously – as the case may be – what 'the future' will bring. Our own actions are embodied in the laws which govern us, but these laws are above us, and we are their slaves. The giant state and economic system are not any more controlled by man. They run wild, and their leaders are like a person on a runaway horse, who is proud of managing to keep in the saddle, even though he is powerless to direct the horse.

What is modern man's *relationship to his fellow man*? It is one between two abstractions, two living machines, who use each other. The employer uses the ones whom he employs; the salesman uses his customers. Everybody is to everybody else a commodity, always to be treated with certain friendliness, because even if he is not of use now, he may be later. There is not much love or hate to be found in human relations of our day. There is, rather, a superficial friendliness, and a more than superficial fairness, but behind that surface is distance and indifference. There is also a good deal of subtle distrust. When one man says to another, 'You speak to John Smith; he is all right,' it is an expression of reassurance against a general distrust. Even love and the relationship between sexes have assumed this character. The great sexual emancipation, as it occurred after the First World War, was a desperate attempt to substitute mutual sexual pleasure for a deeper feeling of love. When this turned out to be a disappointment the erotic polarity between the sexes was reduced to a minimum and replaced by a friendly partnership, a small combine which had amalgamated its forces to hold out better in the daily battle of life, and to relieve the feeling of isolation and aloneness which everybody has.

The alienation between man and man results in the loss of those general and social bonds which characterize medieval as well as most other precapitalist societies. Modern society consists of 'atoms' (if we use the Greek equivalent of 'individual'), little particles estranged from each other but held together by selfish interests and by the necessity to make use of each other. Yet man is a social being with a deep need to share, to help, to feel as a member of a group. What has happened to these social strivings in man? They manifest themselves in the special sphere of the *public* realm, which is strictly separated from the private realm. Our private dealings with our fellow men are governed by the principle of egotism, 'each for himself, God for us all,' in flagrant contradiction to Christian teaching. The individual is motivated by egotistical interest, and not by solidarity with and love for his fellow man. The latter feelings may assert themselves secondarily as private acts of philanthropy or kindness, but they are not part of the basic structure of our social relations. Separated from our private life as individuals is the realm of our social life as 'citizens'. In this realm the State is the embodiment of our social existence; as citizens we are supposed to, and in fact usually do, exhibit a sense of social obligation and duty. We pay taxes, we vote, we respect the laws, and in the case of war we are willing to sacrifice our lives. What clearer example could there be of the separation between private and public existence than the fact that the same man who would not think of spending one hundred dollars to relieve the need of a stranger does not hesitate to risk his life to save this same stranger when in war they both happen to be soldiers in uniform? The uniform is the embodiment of our social nature – civilian garb, of our egotistic nature.

The division between the community and the political state has led to the projection of all social feelings into the State, which thus becomes an idol, a power standing over and above man. Man submits to the State as to the embodiment of his own social feelings, which he worships as powers alienated from himself; in his private life as an individual he suffers from the isolation and aloneness which are the necessary result of this separation. The worship of the State can only disappear if man takes back the social powers into himself, and builds a community in which his social feelings are not something *added* to his private existence, but in which his private and social existence are one and the same.

What is the relationship of *man towards himself*? I have described elsewhere this relationship as 'marketing orientation'. In this orientation, man experiences himself as a thing to be employed successfully on the market. He does not experience himself as an active agent, as the bearer of human powers. He is alienated from these powers. His aim is to sell himself successfully on the market. His sense of self does not stem from his activity as a loving and thinking individual, but from his socio-economic role. If things could speak, a typewriter would answer the question 'Who are you?' by saying 'I am a typewriter', and an automobile, by saying 'I am an automobile', or more specifically by saying, 'I am a Ford', or 'a Buick', or 'a Cadillac'. If you ask a man 'Who are you'? he answers 'I am a manufacturer', 'I am a clerk', 'I am a doctor' – or 'I am a married man', 'I am the father of two kids', and his answer has pretty much the same meaning as that of the speaking *thing* would have. That is the way he experiences himself, not as a man, with love, fear, convictions, doubts, but as that abstraction, alienated from his real nature, which fulfills a certain function in the social system. His sense of value depends on his success: on whether he can sell himself favourably, whether he can make more of himself than he started out with, whether he is a success. His body, his mind and his soul are his capital, and his task in life is to invest it favourably, to make a profit of himself. Human qualities like friendliness, courtesy, kindness, are transformed into commodities, into assets of the 'personality package', conducive to a higher price on the personality market. If the individual fails in a profitable investment of himself, he feels that *he* is a failure; if he succeds, *he* is a succeess. Clearly, his sense of his own value always depends on factors extraneous to himself, on the fickle judgement of the market, which decides about his value as it decides about the value of commodities. He, like all commodities that cannot be sold profitably on the market, is worthless as far as his exchange value is concerned, even though his use value may be considerable.

The alienated personality who is for sale must lose a good deal of the sense of dignity which is so characteristic of man even in most primitive cultures. He must lose almost all sense of self, of himself as a unique and induplicable entity. The sense of self stems from the experience of myself as the subject of *my* experiences, *my* thought, *my* feeling, *my* decision, *my* judgement, *my* action. It presupposes that my experience is my own, and not an alienated one. *Things* have no self and men who have become things can have no self.

One cannot fully appreciate the nature of alienation without considering one specific aspect of modern life: its *routinization*, and the *repression of the awareness of the basic problems of human existence.* We touch here upon a universal problem of life. Man has to earn his daily bread, and this is always a more or less absorbing task. He has to take care of the many time- and energy-consuming tasks of daily life, and he is enmeshed in a certain routine necessary for the fulfillment of these tasks. He builds a social order, conventions, habits and ideas, which help him to perform what is necessary, and to live with his fellow man with a minimum of friction. It is characteristic of all culture that it builds a man-made, artificial world, superimposed on the natural world in which man lives. But man can fulfill himself only if he remains in touch with the fundamental facts of his existence, if he can experience the exaltation of love and solidarity, as well as the tragic fact of his aloneness and of the fragmentary character of his existence. If he is completely enmeshed in the routine and in the artifacts of life, if he cannot see anything but the man-made, commonsense appearance of the world, he loses his touch with and the grasp of himself and the world. We find in every culture the conflict between routine and the attempt to get back to the fundamental realities of existence. To help in this attempt has been one of the functions of art and of religion, even though religion itself has eventually become a new form of routine.

Even the most primitive history of man shows us an attempt to get in touch with the essence of reality by artistic creation. Primitive man is not satisfied with the practical functions of his tools and weapons, but strives to adorn and beautify them, transcending their utilitarian function. Aside from art, the most significant way of breaking through the surface of routine and of getting in touch with the ultimate realities of life is to be found in what may be called by the general term of 'ritual'. I am referring here to ritual in the broad sense of the word, as we find it in the performance of a Greek drama, for instance, and not only to rituals in the narrower religious sense. What was the function of the Greek drama? Fundamental problems of human existence were presented in an artistic and dramatic form, and participating in the dramatic performance, the spectator – though not as a spectator in or modern sense of the consumer – was carried away from the sphere of daily routine and brought in touch with himself as a human being, with the roots of his existence. He touched the ground with his feet, and in this process gained strength by which he was brought back to himself. Whether we think of the Greek drama, the medieval passion play, or an Indian dance, whether we think of Hindu, Jewish or Christian religious rituals, we are dealing with various forms of dramatization of the fundamental problems of human existence, with an *acting out* of the very same problems which are *thought out* in philosophy and theology.

What is left of such dramatization of life in modern culture? Almost nothing. Man hardly ever gets out of the realm of man-made conventions and things, and hardly ever breaks through the surface of his routine, aside from grotesque attempts to satisfy the need for a ritual as we see it practised in lodges and fraternities. The only phenomenon approaching the meaning of a ritual, is the participation of the spectator in competitive sports; here at least, one fundamental problem of human existence is dealt with: the fight between men and the vicarious experience of victory and defeat. But what a primitive and restricted aspect of human existence, reducing the richness of human life to one partial aspect!

If there is a fire, or a car collision in a big city, scores of people will gather and watch. Millions of people are fascinated daily by reportings of crimes and by detective stories. They religiously go to movies in which crime and passion are the two central themes. All this interest and fascination is not simply an expression of bad taste and sensationalism, but of a deep longing for a dramatization of ultimate phenomena of human existence, life and death, crime and punishment, the battle between man and nature. But while Greek drama dealt with these problems on a high artistic and metaphysical level, our modern 'drama' and 'ritual' are crude and do not produce any cathartic effect. All this fascination with competitive sports, crime and passion, shows the need for breaking through the routine surface, but the way of its satisfaction shows the extreme poverty of our solution.

The marketing orientation is closely related to the fact that the *need to exchange* has become a paramount drive in modern man. It is, of course, true that even in a primitive economy based on a rudimentary form of division of labour, men exchange goods with each other within the tribe or among neighbouring tribes. The man who produces cloth exchanges it for grain which his neighbour may have produced, or for sickles or knives made by the blacksmith. With increasing division of labour, there is increasing exchange of goods, but normally the exchange of goods is nothing but a means to an economic end. In capitalistic society *exchanging has become an end in itself*.

DISCUSSION POINTS

1   'If you treat others as things you become a thing yourself.' Discuss.

2   Is there any fundamental difference between worshipping God and worshipping the State or some political leader?

3   'Money means freedom.' 'Money kills freedom.' With which of these views do you agree and why?

4   Do you agree that cars, refrigerators, television sets confer status on the owner? If so, why?

5   'When we eat we "eat" a fantasy, when we drink we "drink" labels.' Discuss what is meant by this and say whether or not you agree with it.

6   Have we become a nation of consumers rather than participators?

7   Do you agree with Fromm that man only wants to see and hear what he is conditioned to want to see and to hear?

8   'If everyone strives for himself on the market, the common good will come of it; order and not anarchy will be the result.' This expresses the view of nineteenth century *laissez-faire* capitalists who argue that the best of all possible worlds results when the State does not interfere in business. Do you agree with this view or do you consider that the State has a duty to protect the weak from exploitation by the strong?

9   Private life and public life can be viewed as two distinct spheres of human activity. A man may act in his private life in contradiction to his publicly-held principles if he so wishes. For example, some Socialists send their children to public schools, some who advocate equal opportunity in education try to use their personal influence to obtain university places for their children, some publicly call for sexual restraint but are privately promiscuous. Are they hypocrites or simply defending their right to live their own lives as they see fit?

10   Is ritual important to man – something with meaning for them – or a meaningless routine in which they become trapped?

PROJECT

The process of alienation, says Fromm, 'is the fact that man does not experience himself as the active bearer of his own power and richness, but as an impoverished "thing", dependent on powers outside himself, on to whom he has projected his living substance.' Build up a series of case histories from literature, biography, film, drama, or from real life, of individuals alienated in this way.

READING

Nausea, Jean-Paul Sartre (Hamish Hamilton, 1962). A penetrating novel by the famous French philosopher/novelist into the psychology of a self-exiled scholar.

Erich Fromm

The Outsider, Albert Camus (Penguin, 1961). A novel, set in French Algeria, about a young clerk whose detachment from life proves fatal.

Roots, Arnold Wesker (Penguin, 1959). The central character of this play, Beatie, finds herself increasingly alienated from her family as she begins to educate herself.

The Loneliness of the Long Distance Runner (W. H. Allen & Co, 1959). Smith, a Borstal boy, in training for a cross-country race against a local public school, dwells upon the bitter grudge he has against the society which put him away. (Also available as a Pan paperback.)

Alienation and Freedom, Robert Blauner (University of Chicago Press, 1964). A sociological study of the worker's situation in a number of major industries.

Michael Kullman

The anti-culture born of despair

from *Universities and Left Review*, Summer 1958

After the Second World War secondary education from eleven to fifteen was made free to all sections of British society. The abolition of fees, it was thought, would successfully remove the main barriers to equal educational opportunity. All those who could show, by passing a series of examinations at the age of eleven, that they were able were free to ascend the educational ladder into the grammar schools and have the chance to go on to higher education and the high-grade jobs which required advanced training. But all the evidence of sociologists suggests that an unusually high proportion of children from working-class backgrounds – even those who passed the eleven-plus tests with distinction – tend to drop out of school at fifteen. Those who fail the eleven-plus and go to secondary modern schools have been found to do progressively worse at mental tests as they move through the schools. There seem to be many reasons for this, but one important reason is the "culture" of the school and how it differs from that of the homes from which most working-class children come. Here is an account of the attitudes Michael Kullman found existing among a class of fourteen-year-old secondary modern pupils.

The face of youth

Segregation is the fundamental principle governing education in this country. Segregation is by parental background and income, governing choice of school. Segregation is by the kind of intelligence measured by the 11 plus. Worst of all, perhaps, is segregation into separate streams at the early age of eight according to expected results in the 11 plus.

Far from ironing out or correcting the class differences of our society, the educational system mirrors and even enhances them. The norms are still set by the private undemocratized sector. The result is the self-perpetuation of a socio-culturally dominant class. Culture continues to be a caste mark, and so to be thought the culture of a class.

The philosophy of the bi-partisan though basically conservative and anti-egalitarian 1944 Education Act has done little to remedy this situation. It rests on the far from progressive myth of opportunity. While allowing the wealthy to continue giving their children a full secondary education as they had done before, it sorts the children of the working class into categories. There are those who are essentially and innately unfit for academic work because of lack of intelligence. These are to be relegated to Secondary Modern schools, there to be 'adapted' to life, presumably so as to suit the needs of their future employers. And there are those who are fit for, and could benefit by further education. These are to be given the key opportunity of going to Grammar schools. (Whether selection is to be carried out by the 11 plus or some more accurate method of precasting, potential performance makes little difference. The outcry against the 11 plus therefore misses the mark. For the underlying premise that among those who cannot afford it there are those who are fit and those who are not fit remains the same.)

Far from reducing class differentials in education, the 1944 Act has succeeded only in composing a new pattern of class tensions upon the existing ones. Whereas the socio-cultural barrier used to lie, roughly, between the privately educated upper- and middle-class, and the state educated lower-middle- and working-class, the 1944 Act has divided the state educated amongst themselves. The intellectual cream has been taken off to grammar school, leaving the rest in a skimmed atmosphere. The universities have been enabled by state scholarships to co-opt a still smaller minority to the socio-economic class of university graduates. Readers are presumably familiar with some of the results: the split heart of the Scholarship Boy.

We complain of the lack of a National Theatre, of the paltriness of Arts Council grants, of the ravages of commercialism in art. We deplore much of the content of the mass media. Yet we have no answer to the justification offered that it is what the people want, save to say that the people could be made to want something better. We live in a society that lets culture be the appanage of the minority. Art, poetry, philosophy are by and for the few. Few have had the education to appreciate the finest things in our cultural heritage and these things are resented and rejected by those who have not. Few amongst the best educated really desire to share their culture, because an appreciation of the finest things has come to be a caste mark whose significance would be lost if it were more widely shared. Our culture itself suffers from this. Much of our present-day music, our painting, our poetry, our philosophy, has the obscurity, the sophistication or the second order character of a set of messages couched in the code of a cultural élite. It is not meant for mankind. Much of the best in broadcasting is not put over the Home or the Light, it comes over the Third and is introduced by the monotone of the don. It is addressed to Oxbridge in diaspora. It has been argued recently that what I have called culture is in fact a class culture, and that the great failing of our education system is that it tries to transmit upper-class culture to working-class children. I do not think that there is any alternative to Bach, El Greco, and Shakespeare worth transmitting. I cannot agree with a secondary modern child who preferred the washboard to the harp. Rock and roll may be a substitute for country dancing but not for ballet. I believe there is one human cultural heritage which is only accidentally the appanage of a class. And I believe that the process of getting the education to partake of it must needs be costly and long.

Mozart off a short pier

I once asked a set of fourteen-year-olds in a secondary modern school to write about the kind of music they disliked. I told them to give reasons, but refused to give them any further guidance. They wrote against everything they had been taught by their music master. They wrote about Mozart and Beethoven and Schubert. Fourteen out of thirty-two singled out as object of their special hatred opera. Some gave aesthetic reasons. Classical music was 'slow', 'went on for hours', had 'no go' in it, was full of high notes, had no melody, or rhythm. Others gave reason that gave telling indication of what they expected of art. You could not 'clap your hands' to it, 'jive to it' or even 'hand jive to it'. It had no beat. It did not 'send you'. Then came sociological reasons. Classical music was hated because those who liked it were 'old fogies' or 'squares'. Those who went to operas 'talked posho' or were 'queers'. Brahms was an 'old fogy', Beethoven a 'downright square'! 'Symphonies gave one headaches.' 'Opera singers should be done in', 'Opera banned'. Two children thought Covent Garden and Sadler's Wells ought to be bombed. 'Violin players must hate cats because they make them go up the wall.' 'Beethoven and all his followers are just lucky they are not living today. He would have been chivved up by some cool cats.' 'Mozart ought to take a long run off a short pier.' It is easy to laugh at such answers. It is not so easy to laugh at their violence. They were meant, and written with great diligence. The entire class rose to the occasion. The answers point to something more seriously wrong than the teaching of music in secondary modern schools.

We are the 'squares' and we are hated for not 'getting in the groove' with them, for failing to 'get the message' from Elvis Presley. And the cultural and artistic heritage that we seek to impart is rejected for what we get from it and they cannot. We are hated for 'getting in the groove' with Bach and Bach is hated because we get *our* message from him. I explored the subject further by getting classes to write about 'squares', and to tell me the difference between a 'posh' person and a 'square'. Time and time again I got the same circle of reasons. Classical music was disliked because it was liked by a certain class of people which class of people was disliked because they liked classical music. The 'square' was seldom differentiated from the 'posh' person save that the latter had the additional attributes of talking 'posho' or 'nice', being 'rich' and 'la de da'. This showed the degree to which even secondary modern children are conscious of the correlation between education that makes one a 'square' and socio-economic status that makes one 'posh'. From all this two things emerge and the two are to my mind intimately interrelated. On the one hand a violent dislike for a culture felt to be a class culture and on the other hand a pressing need to 'get sent', taking the form of a cult of 'rock 'n' roll'. Almost every paper I collected was literally strewn with the hallowed names of Elvis Presley, and Tommy Steele, almost invariably in block capitals, and how these artists 'sent' them.

The culture represented by the music of Bach and of Mozart is not disliked simply because it 'belongs' to some remote set of people who attend the Edinburgh Festival and spend money on classical records. The 'square' is not necessarily hated for being 'posh'. Nor is his culture hated solely because it belongs to the rich. Indeed, the rare 'posh' person who is not a 'square' is in a perverse way looked up to and admired: to wit, the Duke of Edinburgh. The 'square' is hated above all for not sharing the secondary modern child's need to 'get sent'. The standard definition of the square was a person who either disliked 'rock and roll' or liked to listen to classical music and read books. But the auxiliary definitions I got were in many cases far more revealing. Thus a 'square' was 'old-fashioned', 'conceited', 'a bore', and more significantly still, 'a person who does not approve what you do' and a person 'who lets you down'. The 'square' is essentially out of touch with what the children feel to be their needs. And the culture that he represents is hated because it cannot be participated in, and corresponds to no inner need. 'You cannot jive to it,' and jiving is a way of 'getting sent', 'you *cannot even* clap your hands to it'. It is completely unfunctional. And this provides a rationale for their dislike. Anti-culture is with the majority of secondary modern children I have questioned a complete and closed system. It is a set of strong emotional attitudes about culture completed by a set of justifications. The culture teachers are attempting to impart is both something 'old fogies get stuck up about' and something that could not possibly 'send' anyone. It is meaningless pretence. Needless to say secondary modern children are mistaken. 'Squares' too need to 'get sent'. For 'squares' are human too. I firmly believe that so long as society is at all imperfect escapism is a basic human right. The question is whether or not escapism should take so destructive a form.

The vacuum third

I have tried above to give some account of the philosophy of what teachers have variously described to me as 'teen-age nihilism' or the 'vacuum mind'. I have taken as a starting point what they think of music but I believe it to be pretty obvious that the same attitudes extend to most of the subjects taught in secondary modern schools. Formal education beyond bare literacy to read comic strips has to them no use, corresponds to no inner need. Secondary modern staff and pupils frequently share the same despair, a sense of the uselessness of attempting to teach on the one hand, and on the other a sense of the uselessness of school. This leads to uncontrollable classes and nervous breakdowns amongst the staff. Many are the classrooms in which teachers and pupils feel alike imprisoned.

I remember how when I was at a posh little prep school my erstwhile friends and I used to provoke those less privileged than ourselves, whom we used to term 'gutter-snipes' and 'street urchins', to battle with us on our way home from school. We had no common language. It was inconceivable to us that we should play with them. I remember

51

quite vividly how at my public school we used to complain of having to row against grammar schools. We felt grammar schools to be upstarts and parvenus. That grammar schools should dream of taking up rowing was a challenge to be resisted at all costs. Sometimes they would beat us. We were easily consoled for, after all, 'they were not gentlemen'. During my five years at a public school I do not once recall having to do with anyone who did not go to a private or at any rate a grammar school. Seventy-five per cent of our contemporaries and fellow citizens were regarded as humanly beyond the pale. We were not taught snobbery; we were brought up in a tradition. And those of us who sided with Labour in political arguments incurred wrath not because Labour policies were a menace to our fathers' incomes but because they were quite literally class traitors. I cite my own example because I do not consider it all untypical. Research should, of course, be carried out into class attitudes amongst 'ruling class' children. To this there are obvious obstacles on the part of private school authorities. For to ask children questions about class attitudes is to raise questions about something taken for granted.

The questionnaire

Taking a look at the other side of the social picture, we questionnaired a number of secondary modern children on what they thought respectively of grammar school and public school children. The question about grammar school children generated the most violent answers. They were characterized as 'snobs', 'big heads', people who 'went around as though they owned the place', and as thinking 'they had all the brains and no-one else had'. Some put 'rats' and 'scum'. The question about public schools was as often as not misunderstood. Public schools seemed to be taken to mean state schools. Some put 'alright', others 'easy to get on with', or 'nice kids'. Where the difference was explained most people put 'don't know any', a few put 'snobs'. A thirteen-year-old remarked 'pity they are snobs for they are at the best schools'. The attitudes towards grammar school children of those in non-grammar streams of comprehensive schools were far more moderate. These ranged from 'brainy' through 'a little stuck up' to 'lucky'. Those in grammar streams of comprehensive schools were as was to be expected a little more conscious of what was meant by public schools, and almost always put 'snobs' regardless of the fact they did not know any. Daily contact between grammar and non-grammar

...s in comprehensive schools may help lessen the bitterness born
...f II plus. It is to this extent a partial solution. But the answers we got
to a further question 'What do you think of those of your own age
already at work?' shows how much of a problem still remains. Whereas
fourteen- and fifteen-year-olds in non-grammar schools tended to
express envy, those in grammar streams tended to express sympathetic
condescension. The former said 'lucky', 'they've got the money'; the
latter said 'nice but ignorant', 'silly not to stay on' (as though it was up
to them!), 'they are unlucky', and even 'good luck to them'.

The questionnaire used to obtain some of the information here contained a number of questions intended to ascertain class differentials in
expectations and attitudes. Children were asked a number of multiple
choice questions about how they got on with parents, how they got on
with teachers, how much spare time they spent at home and whether
they found life at school worthwhile, which they had to answer in terms
of five possibilities. They were also asked a number of open-ended
questions such as 'What do you most look forward to in the next few
years?', 'What do you think you will be doing at the age of 30?' and
'What, if different, would you like to be doing at the age of 30?'

These were followed by 'Do you think you will get sufficient education to do what you would really like to do in life?' and 'If not, why not?
Who do you think to blame?'.

We have as yet obtained only 70 answers, with one exception confined to fourteen- and fifteen-year-olds at comprehensive schools
(including grammar streams) and secondary modern schools. So it is too
early to draw any but the most tentative conclusions. We hope in the
none-too-distant future to obtain a sufficiently large random sample
from all classes to form a somewhat better picture.

A preliminary glance at results so far received shows a surprising
difference between the attitudes and expectations of, on the one hand,
secondary modern and non-grammar stream children in comprehensive
schools, and grammar stream children on the other. The former rarely
if ever find school more than fairly worthwhile. They look forward
above all to making money and leaving school. They have a nebulous
idea, if any, of what they will be doing at the age of 30. They seem to
have a very limited time perspective and in answer to 'What gives you
most satisfaction in day-to-day life?' tend to put 'girls' or even 'sex'.

They tend to get on 'very well' with their parents, but tend to spend
'little' to 'as little as possible' of their spare time at home. They seldom
think they will not have sufficient education to do what they would

really like to do. Grammar stream children tend to have a more realistic picture of what they will be doing at 30. As often as not they find life at school 'very' worthwhile. 'What do you dread most in life?' sometimes gets the answer 'GCE'. They tend as is only to be expected to spend a little more time at home, and frequently put 'a good day's work' or 'doing a job well and getting praised for it' for the question about what gives them most satisfaction in their day-to-day life. The impression one gets is that the 'grammar stream' child is if anything more ambitious than his contemporary in the non-grammar stream, and that he lives his life in a more extended time perspective.

A complete human life

More general questions such as 'What do you think bad, wrong or unjust about England and the English way of life?' and 'Do you think there is anything you could help do about it?' showed up little difference between grammar stream and non-grammar stream children. Answers to the former question were sometimes 'irrelevant' but revealing, as for instance, 'The old pro's of Piccadilly', 'the Niggers and the Jews', though there were occasional glimpses of acute social consciousness, 'one law for the rich and one for the poor', 'slums' or 'the schools'. The answer to the latter question 'Do you think there is anything you could help do about it?' was inevitably 'no'. This is where the old class difference between the state educated and the privately educated is very significant. Though we have not had any yet, I am sure we shall get relatively more affirmative answers from those at public schools. When I was fifteen two boys out of a class of twenty at my public school wanted to become MPs and one a minister, though, of course, public school boys have less immediate and personal reasons for finding things wrong with English society. Working class children's answers seem to point to a certain apathy. Of the seventy answers we have had sixty-five intended to vote Labour, three Communist and two Conservative, but only ten thought they could do something about what was wrong, the majority did not bother to answer, some twenty put 'no'. Those who answered 'yes' frequently advocated violence, as one who thought 'the yids' the bad thing about England and advocated throwing them out, or else gave stupid answers such as 'put me in charge'. None saw the answer in terms of political action via the Labour Party. In answer to the somewhat vague question, 'Are you happy in life', the vast majority answered 'very'. Of course those so far questioned were all very young.

...at right have we to speak of the despair of those considered 'unfit' for proper secondary education? In a narrowly empirical sense none at all. Secondary modern children are happy for they will soon be at work. And if they hate Shakespeare and love 'rock and roll' let them – *de gustibus non est disputandum*, so long as their gangs do not harm our property. It seems as though we were using despair in a Kierkegaardian sense; we are all in despair whether we feel it or not, for in the face of God we are all sinners. But this is not so. There is something metaphysical in the concept of despair I have been presupposing here, yet it can be measured. It can be measured not by straight-forward nose-counting of those who will say yes to 'Are you in despair?', but by counting the number of those showing certain symptoms. I have tried in this article to sketch certain symptoms. Anti-culture in secondary modern schools, and the accompanying focus on short-run economic and sexual achievement is but one of these. But the disease is a psycho-social one affecting all classes and age groups, and the ivory towerism of the Third Programme or of the back pages of the *New Statesman* are further symptoms. The disease is dangerously self-perpetuating. Acceptance of the philosophy of the 1944 Act, acceptance of the theory that proper secondary education should be reserved to a minority selected by parental income and/or 11 plus, is today producing a generation made unfit for proper secondary education, and who are unlikely to demand it for their children. Proper secondary education I believe to be a pre-condition of participation in a fully human life, and as such a human right. Until a far greater number have had it it will not be demanded as a human right, and will remain the privilege of a social class extended to the lucky few. And it will not be in the interests of the minority of the decently educated to seek the universalization of something that is now their privilege. Such are the mechanics of cultural alienation as operated by our educational system today. Millions are spent daily in state schools forming children made unfit, human beings who feel that proper education and the culture that is a significant part of its content is not for them. Children are made not to care for what society owes them. This need not be so, but it is unlikely that the next Labour government will succeed in breaking this vicious circle. For the majority of its supporters were forced to work in their early teens, its MPs, its thinkers and its leaders belong willy-nilly to those who can afford the best schools. And the trade union chiefs do not care except in so far as raising school leaving age affects the market for labour.

The despair that plagues our society is despair about the possibility of

Michael Kullman

a complete human life for all. It affects intellectual and secondary modern child alike. The former have to offer what the latter is being formed to refuse. Those who have seen cultural alienation in operation at close range in our secondary modern schools, those who have tried to teach there and failed to accept the dirty white lie about there being the fit and the unfit, those know they have plenty in common with the children. At the end of the long day's boredom and strain both terribly need to 'get sent'. Both could share something else: the culture that might be transmitted. But that is reserved for other schools and another type of child. A human life for some is not a fully human life for anyone. The violent teddy boy, the pathologically shy northern chemist, and the blasé public school boy, each in his way a victim, are all symptoms of the same disease. They will not speak to each other for they cannot.

DISCUSSION POINTS

1 'Everyone can get on today if they have the ability.' Discuss.

2 'There is no such thing as social class in Britain today.' This is a commonly held view. In your experience is it true?

3 How can the educational system 'mirror' class differences?

4 'Mozart ought to take a long run off a short pier.' This view expresses a violent rejection of so-called high culture. Is there any justification for feeling so strongly about traditional music?

5 How do you feel about the view that high culture – art, opera, theatre, poetry, symphony music, ballet – is only for the middle- and upper-classes; other people are incapable of appreciating it and should get pop culture in school and from the mass media.

6 'The individual always knows what's best for himself.' Discuss.

7 'Public and grammar schools produce snobs and should therefore be abolished.' Do you agree?

8 'An extended education is limiting. The earlier one escapes into work the more freedom one enjoys in life.' What do you think of this view?

9 What is bad, wrong or unjust about Britain and the British way of life and do you think there is anything you could help to do about it?

10   Should pupils in schools have a greater say in what they are taught or not?

PROJECT

Write to a number of secondary schools – grammar, modern and comprehensive – requesting permission to interview a cross-section of school-leavers. Devise a questionnaire intended to discover the kinds of views Michael Kullman was examining. Include some of the questions he used. Compare your own results with his. How do attitudes differ between schools and between pupils in different streams within schools – if these exist.

READING

The Uses of Literacy, Richard Hoggart (Penguin, 1958). An account of the impact of literacy on working-class culture based largely on the author's childhood experience in a northern industrial city.

Education and the Working Class, Brian Jackson and Dennis Marsden (Penguin, 1966). A study comparing the school lives and subsequent careers of a group of middle-class and a group of working-class boys in a northern city.

The Sociology of the School, Marten Shipman (Longmans, 1968). A sociologist looks at the ways in which the organization and culture of schools may influence their pupils.

The Secondary Modern School, William Taylor (Faber, 1963). A history and criticism of the secondary modern school by a sociologist.

Albert Angelo, B. S. Johnson (Constable, 1964). A novel based on the author's experience of teaching in a particularly tough London secondary modern school. Other books based on similar experiences include

To Sir With Love, by E. R. Braithwaite (Four Square, 1967) and *Roaring Boys*, by Edward Blishen (Panther, 1966).

The Comprehensive School, Robin Pedley (Penguin, 1963). An account of a kind of school which could eventually replace the secondary modern.

The Grammar School, Robin Davis (Penguin, 1968).

The Hothouse Society, Royston Lambert (OUP, 1968). A fascinating study by a sociologist of life in the country's most exclusive schools.

E

J. A. C. Brown

Truth drugs and lie detectors

from *The Techniques of Persuasion*, Penguin 1963

The rise of modern totalitarian states like Nazi Germany and the Soviet Union, and the means employed by them to gain conformity, have resulted in a great deal of attention being paid to methods of controlling men's minds. In the following passage from J. A. C. Brown's book *The Techniques of Persuasion*, some of the methods for eliciting 'confessions' from suspects are described.

Psychotherapy is directed towards the modification or change of faulty attitudes and is a somewhat elastic term which includes anything from mere suggestion with or without hypnosis, where the intention is simply to increase the patient's confidence and so enable him to face his problems, to analytic psychotherapy, where the intention is to break down old attitudes and allow them to be replaced by new ones more close to reality.

Psychoanalysis, the method of therapy devised by Freud, is the most thoroughgoing of these analytic procedures and also, unfortunately, the most prolonged, necessitating fifty-five minutes every day for five days a week over a period of two or more years. During these sessions the patient lies on a couch and is asked to talk at random, saying whatever comes into his head no matter what its nature, and in due course the free association leads to the basic sources of conflict which are, of course, unconscious. The patient has come to the analyst with various symptoms such as irrational fears or phobias, attacks of uncontrollable anxiety, insomnia, and the like, but these are regarded as being the result of underlying conflicts which arise basically from defects in inter-personal relations. The aim of analysis is to bring such conflicts into consciousness so that they can be dealt with at the rational level in a practical manner. In this process the patient's attitude towards the analyst, the transference, plays a leading part; for it is this attitude which, as it were, forms a representative sample of his faulty attitudes towards significant figures in his early life when the basic conflicts arose. The analyst points out the irrational nature of these attitudes, previously not fully realized by the patient, and the early problems are acted out in relation to the analyst and in this way finally lose their compulsive nature. Since complete psychoanalysis is out of reach to most people for practical reasons of time, money, and general suitability of the method in a given case, attempts have been made to shorten analysis which have for the most part been in one or other of two directions: either an attempt is made to reach the conflicts in the un-conscious by means of short cuts such as the use of drugs or hypnosis, or the interpretation of the analyst is active – i.e., knowing on the basis of his knowledge of psychopathology and the general clinical picture what the patient's conflicts are, he will force them upon the patient's attention without waiting for them to appear gradually in free associat-ion. Such methods are quite satisfactory when the onset of the neurosis is relatively recent and in direct response to some fairly severe provoca-tion from the environment, or in cases which are monosymptomatic as when the most obvious problem is a single phobia. In fact, they approximate to those used by Freud in the early days of the movement, when a symptom was regarded as the tombstone marking the spot where a traumatic memory lay repressed. Later evidence, however, made it clear that neurosis is a disorder of the total personality even if on cursory examination only a single symptom can be observed, and it is generally accepted that removing a symptom in this way is not in itself tantamount to cure any more than suppressing a troublesome cough is a cure for bronchitis. However, in an otherwise good per-sonality it may be regarded as a satisfactory result, especially if the environmental stress was severe and is unlikely to be met with again. For this reason such short methods are specially useful in battle neurosis where a terrifying memory has been repressed with resultant symptom-formation. In such cases the patient is given an injection of Pentothal (thiopentone sodium), sodium amytal, or scopolamine which makes him drowsy enough for repression to be relaxed and the memory is brought into consciousness, producing great emotional upset whilst the traumatic incident is re-lived. This emotional crisis is known as abreaction and is therapeutic to the degree that the patient is able to accept the rejected material and integrate it into his ego as past of part history. It is then no longer an undigested mass causing symptoms by reason of repression, but a formerly traumatic memory which has been made a part of consciously-recalled experience and integrated into the rest of the patient's awareness. Similar results may be obtained by the use of ether anaesthesia or hypnosis and the same methods are frequently employed in everyday practice to make a patient aware of his or her problems when they have been partly or wholly repressed. By these means the period of analysis is greatly shortened, although the best results are obtained, as already indicated, in people of previous good personality who have been under considerable environmental stress.

Drugs employed in this way are, of course, what are popularly known as 'truth drugs', and it is necessary to consider how far they are, or can be, employed for other than therapeutic reasons. Can they be used, for example, to extract the truth from unwilling prisoners, whether political or otherwise? All the evidence suggests the contrary. Can they be used, on the other hand, to cause prisoners to make false confessions, as was frequently suggested during the Soviet purges of the nineteen-thirties? Certainly they cannot. The so-called 'truth drugs' are simply ordinary anaesthetics most of which have been in use for many years (ether, widely believed to be the most effective of all in psychiatry, is actually the oldest, dating back to 1847) and in sub-anaesthetic doses they produce much the same effect as amounts of alcohol sufficient to lead to drunkenness. That is to say, they relax conscious control and enable the individual to speak without his usual censorship coming into action. Their use is based on the ancient, if not entirely true, saying: '*In vino veritas*.' Fortunately or unfortunately, as everyone knows, drunkenness does not necessarily cause everyone to tell the objective truth in terms of external reality, otherwise we should not so frequently be exposed to the drunkard's fantasies of how badly he is treated at home and how he was instrumental in winning the last war, or the war before the last. What the good psychologist learns is a great deal of truth not about objective happenings but about the character of the individual himself. This suits the psychiatrist very well, for in the sense that matters to him everything his patient says is 'true' in so far as it reveals his real attitudes to life. When, in his early years, Freud listened to his patients' accounts of how they had been sexually seduced in childhood by near relatives and subsequently found that these happenings were fabricated and had never really happened in the vast majority of cases, he was at first perplexed. But finally he came to realize that the important thing was not whether or not they had happened but rather that the patient felt as if they had.

But this kind of 'truth' is of no use at all to the political investigator who wants to catch his prisoner out and, unfortunately for him, no drug exists which can compel an unwilling victim to tell the truth. The evidence given under the influence of 'truth drugs' is admitted in certain American courts of law provided the accused is willing to undergo the test, but it is well-known that people can lie just as effectively under the influence of a drug as without it and, even when his censorship is relaxed, a prisoner who is on his guard is able to stick to his original story. He may, indeed, have got to the stage where he largely believes it himself. Patients are more susceptible to the influence of such drugs because they are usually ready to co-operate with the psychiatrist in order to lose their symptoms; but even in these instances objective recall is not always possible. 'Truth drugs' have no magical or inevitable power and the writer well remembers a soldier who, during the last war, was able to maintain for more than two years that he did not know his name, unit, birthplace, or any other facts about his past life, in spite of every therapeutically permissible attempt to discover them.

The lie-detector is another method sometimes employed in American criminal practice, being based, first, on Jung's original word-association test for discovering the nature of unconscious complexes, and, secondly, on the long-familiar principle that telling a lie ordinarily leads to anxiety, which can be demonstrated by the physical changes it produces in the body. This fact was allegedly employed by the police of Eastern countries, who, on obtaining a number of suspects, would ask them all to masticate and swallow a small amount of dry rice, the guilty person being recognized by the fact that with the dry mouth of fear he was unable to carry out the order. In the Jung word-association test, occasionally employed in psychiatry, a list of one hundred words is read out slowly to the testee, who is asked to respond with the first word that comes into his head, the reaction time (i.e. the time taken to reply) and the word given in response being noted by the psychiatrist. Most of the words are neutral ones but certain key words are introduced relating to subjects over which conflicts often arise, and a delay in responding or an unusual association often gives a clue to the patient's complexes. The lie detector employs a similar list which includes amongst the neutral words others the significance of which could only be meaningful to one who had been acquainted with the circumstances of the crime. Meanwhile, instead of relying upon such data as the reaction time and unusual response, the investigator has the testee connected up with a battery of instruments which are capable of indicating anxiety through an increased pulse-rate, raised blood-pressure, increased sweating of the skin, and so on. Thus a robber, confronted by the name of an article which he alone could know was among the stolen goods, may give himself away by his concealed anxiety as revealed by the instruments. This method is now little used in psychiatry but doubtless has some limited application in criminology although even here nobody can be convicted on the evidence of the lie-detector alone, and if the suspect sticks to his story he is in little more danger than formerly.

DISCUSSION POINTS

1   In what ways does the author suggest that psychoanalysis can 'free' a patient from his neuroses?

2   Brown says that complete psychoanalysis is out of reach to most people for practical reasons of time, money and general suitability of the method in a given case. If a particular method of treatment is best for a sick person is it right that lack of money should prevent him from obtaining it? Do you take the view that medical treatment should be paid for by the patient, or is this something which the State should make freely available to *all* its citizens?

3   Should people who are mentally ill be treated as dangerous?

4   Discuss the view that drugs should only be used for therapeutic purposes and that their use by the authorities to elicit the truth from suspects is an infringement of personal liberty.

5   Should the courts accept confessions elicited by 'truth drugs' as valid evidence?

6   Can you think of other scientific methods which the police employ which are generally accepted? Why are these more acceptable to the public than the methods Brown discusses?

PROJECT

A number of books, both fiction and non-fiction, include accounts of persuasion techniques used to undermine human liberty. Read one of the books on the subject written by psychologists and compare it with either a fictional account or with a film obviously attempting to persuade the viewer.

READING

The Techniques of Persuasion, J. A. C. Brown (Penguin, 1963).

Battle For The Mind, William Sargant (Pan, 1959).

Thought Reform and the Psychology of Totalism, Robert J. Lifton (Penguin, 1967).

Brainwashing in Red China, E. Hunter (Vanguard Press, New York, 1955).

The Captive Mind, C. Milosz (Secker & Warburg, 1953).

Fiction

Nineteen Eighty-Four, George Orwell (Penguin, 1954).

Darkness At Noon, Arthur Koestler (Penguin, 1940).

The Trial, Franz Kafka (Secker & Warburg, 1945; Penguin, 1953).

FILMS

The Russian Miracle. A fascinating propaganda film which tells the story of the Soviet Union from before the Revolution of 1917 until the launching of the first Sputnik. Note the clever use of music and slanted commentary.

Billy Graham Crusade films. The films of Graham's crusades are almost textbook examples of the propaganda techniques outlined in the works of J. A. C. Brown and William Sargant referred to above.

Films of the Nuremberg rallies of the Nazis, made in the 1930s by Leni Riefenstahl show not dissimilar techniques employed for a far more sinister end.

The Mind-Benders. A film not used for persuasion itself, but showing the horrifying effect of research techniques on a human guinea-pig, himself a scientist.

National Council for Civil Liberties
Arrest

As a society becomes more complex and the growth of technology accelerates there is a tendency for more and more power to be exercised over the individual's daily life by centralized government. This is usually justified by reference to the need for greater control and greater efficiency. In Britain, where individuals are very proud of their civil liberties, one of the most difficult problems is how to maintain good relations between the police and the public. The pamphlet *Arrest*, published by the National Council for Civil Liberties, describes the rights of the individual citizen and the powers of the police in making an arrest.

Good relations between the police and the public depend on mutual confidence and knowledge of the rights and powers of both. The police have a difficult and responsible task which is not made easier if members of the public refuse to co-operate because they are unsure of their position. This booklet is published in an endeavour to set out the rights of the public and the powers of the police when an arrest is made. We hope it will contribute to better understanding and co-operation.

The booklet has been prepared by members of our legal panel and others with close experience of the police. In addition, we are glad to acknowledge the help we have received from the Albany Trust in preparing and publishing this guide to our rights.

NATIONAL COUNCIL FOR CIVIL LIBERTIES
4 Camden High Street, London NW1. Telephone: 387 2544

1 Arrest without warrant

There is a wide range of offences for which a policeman can lawfully arrest you without any warrant from a magistrate. It is impossible to know what these are without prolonged study – their gravity, for example, affords no guide whatever – but you are not expected to know them all. If a policeman tells you he is arresting you, *ask him what for*, as he is bound to tell you. Note carefully what he says, take his number (if he is in uniform) and 'go quietly'. If his action is unlawful, your remedy comes later.

2

If a policeman asks you to 'accompany him to the station' and you don't want to go, ask him whether he is arresting you. (He may be uncertain whether an arrest would be lawful or not.) If he says no, you are free to do as you wish. More often than not it will save you subsequent trouble if you go.

3 Arrest with warrant

If a policeman has a magistrate's warrant to arrest you, ask to see it; if the warrant relates to a civil debt, e.g. non-payment of maintenance or rates, it must be produced on arrest; but if it is a warrant to arrest you for an alleged offence, a policeman need not have it with him – the law requires only that the warrant shall be in existence – but it must be shown or read to you, whichever you prefer, as soon after your arrest as possible. Make sure that it really means you, and see whether it says that you are to be released on bail.

4 Bail

Unless the warrant says you are to have bail, the police have no power to grant it. But when the police arrest you *without* a warrant – and this is more usual – they *may*, in any circumstances, release you on bail, and they *must* if it will be 24 hours before they can bring you before a magistrate. There are exceptions to this. You won't usually get bail if the offence alleged against you is 'a serious one'; nor, if you are under 17, will you get it if it is thought necessary to remove you from bad company or that your release would 'defeat the ends of justice'. In any event, bail does not usually (in England and Wales) mean bringing cash to the police station or court; it means satisfying the police that you have saleable property to the value of the amount required. If the police require a sum of bail which is 'prohibitive', they are acting unlawfully, but this is a wrong for which they can be called to account only by way of a High Court action when the criminal case is over. Meanwhile you can apply to a High Court Judge for immediate bail.

5 *Questioning*

You are not bound to answer any police questions whatsoever. (You can be required by law to tell the police who was driving your car at a particular time, and fined if you refuse; but this is normally done by correspondence and seldom arises in the case of someone under arrest.) If, however, you decide to answer no questions, it is better to declare 'I do not wish to say anything until I have seen my solicitor' than to remain absolutely silent. In court, silence may sometimes be regarded as having signified agreement with or acceptance of something the police or other witnesses were saying at the time. And it can (though it shouldn't) make the case against you *seem* stronger by creating an atmosphere unfavourable to you, in which it is much easier for the prosecution witnesses to appear franker and more convincing than you do.

If you have been charged, questions relating to the offence may only be asked when it is necessary 'for the purpose of preventing or minimising harm or loss to some other person or to the public or for clearing up an ambiguity in a previous answer or statement'. The police must, however, caution you again before asking such questions (see para. 12).

6 *Statements*

A statement may either be written personally or dictated to a police officer who must write down the exact words spoken, may not prompt, and may only ask such questions as are necessary to make the statement coherent. It should be signed as being quite voluntary and true, and all police officers present should countersign it.

Foreigners may make a statement in their own language and should sign that copy which is in their own language.

7 *Seeing a lawyer*

If you decide to have a lawyer, don't sign anything until he comes.

When he comes, you are entitled to talk to him out of anyone else's hearing, though a policeman will probably keep you in sight to see that you do not try to escape.

8 *Contacting relatives*

Insist on using the telephone, unless a telegram would be cheaper because of the distance, to give any essential message to your lawyer, your family or friends. You will understand that the police telephone is busy and that your use of it will have to be brief and minimal. The police will supply you with writing materials on request, and your letter or message will be posted, or sent by other means, e.g. by telegram or by cab, usually at your expense.

9

The police will sometimes – and exceptionally – allow you to see relatives or friends while you are in a cell, but these interviews, unlike those with your lawyer, will NOT be private; the conversation will be listened to, and no articles will be allowed to change hands.

10 *Fingerprinting*

The police may want to take your fingerprints. Whatever the offence for which you are charged, you are entitled to refuse, and to take them without your consent would be an assault. If you refuse, the police can ask the court to order that your fingerprints be taken without your consent; and if the court so orders, it can then be done either at the court or at a remand prison. The fingerprints of an arrested person will sometimes help the police in the investigation of a crime, but more frequently their purpose is to ascertain, from the Central Finger Print Registry, whether the arrested person has been convicted and finger-printed before. (The National Council for Civil Liberties considers that fingerprints should only be taken in connection with offences where prints might be relevant.)

11 *Charging*

When you have been formally charged at the station, the police should hand you a form containing the precise details of the charge against you and a statement (in accordance with the 'Judges' Rules') that you are not obliged to make any answer. Since they are not required *by law* to do this, it is not a right which you can enforce, or in default of which you can obtain subsequent redress; but you should note carefully whether it is done.

12 Cautioning

A police officer must caution you concerning questioning and the making of statements as soon as he has sufficient evidence to suspect you of having committed an offence. The caution, according to the Judges' Rules, should be in these words:

'You are not obliged to say anything unless you wish to do so, but what you say may be put into writing and given in evidence.'

A second caution, on being charged, is much the same.

There is a third form of caution which must be given if the police wish to ask questions after you have been charged. These words should be:

'I wish to put some questions to you about the offence with which you you have been charged. You are not obliged to answer any of these quest-ions, but if you do the questions and answers will be taken down in writing and may be given in evidence.'

It is a mistake to think that any failure to give a caution *necessarily* makes a prisoner's statement inadmissible at his trial. Its use adds weight to any damaging admissions that he may have made; its omission may not destroy their value. What does destroy their value is any police suggestion to the prisoner that 'it will be better for him' to 'make a clean breast of it', *or better for anyone else. Involving others cannot possibly help you; the police have absolutely no authority to strike these bargains, to fulfil any promise, to offer any inducement or undertaking, or to carry out any threat.*

13 Searching the person

Once you are charged, the police have a Common Law right to search your pockets, bags, etc., for articles that may have some bearing on the offence charged against you, or with which you might do some injury to yourself or others while in police custody. Other articles in your possession, INCLUDING THIS BOOKLET, you are entitled to retain. You will be asked to sign a list of the things taken from you, and to sign it again when they are returned to you.

14 Searching premises

Neither the police nor anyone else is entitled to search your house, shop or other premises without a 'search warrant' from a magistrate. The magistrate who gives it need not be sitting in court – he might be in his own home. You are entitled to see the warrant; therefore the policeman (unlike the one arresting you – see No. 3) must have it on him or he cannot lawfully come in. If, having seen it, you refuse to allow entry, the police can break in – and they will. If they have no warrant and you refuse them entry, they will probably post policemen outside the place until they can get a warrant, which might take some hours. If you are totally innocent, you may then have a legal right to sue the police for defaming your character in the estimation of neighbours.

15 Evidence in court

You are *not* bound to give evidence at your trial. You will probably be told in court that you are entitled *either* to make a statement without going into the witness-box, in which event no-one may ask you any questions about what you say; *or* to go into the witness-box and give sworn evidence, in which event you can be questioned, though not in such a way as to damage your character. The truth is that if you wish you can do both these things, and it is sometimes an advantage to do so.

16 Police warrant card

The Commissioner of Police has refused to provide us with a sample (cancelled) police warrant card. We are therefore unable to reproduce here a facsimile of what every police officer on duty (in uniform or plain clothes) has to carry with him as his certificate of authority. In London it is a folding piece of black leather-covered board measuring 3 inches by 2 inches when folded. Some provincial police warrant cards do not fold, are kept in a transparent plastic envelope, and bear the photograph of the holder. All warrant cards bear the policeman's name and number, whether or not he is a plain clothes officer and whatever his rank. Make a note of the number if you can.

Bogus plain clothes policemen sometimes purport to show police warrant cards to people they surprise in compromising circumstances, and then extort money or valuables from them as a condition of refraining from arrest or prosecution. Similarly, bogus policemen have abducted persons in cars, or accosted persons at night to search their belongings, and then stolen the contents or assaulted the person concerned.

Should anyone ever attempt to do this to you, insist on his going with you to the nearest police station or uniformed policeman, and report the matter immediately. The warrant card is intended to identify the policeman.

17 Remember

The Police MUST

Tell you at the earliest possible moment what offence you are charged with.

If arresting you on a magistrate's warrant, show you the warrant as soon after your arrest as practicable.

Allow you to communicate with, telephone or telegraph your family or your solicitor immediately after you have been arrested.

Allow you to talk to your solicitor out of their hearing.

They CANNOT

Compel you to accompany them to the police station unless they have arrested you.

Compel you to answer any questions or to sign any statement.

Hold out any inducement or make any promise or threat in order to extract a statement from you. Any statement obtained by such means may be ruled inadmissible by the court.

Compel you to have your fingerprints taken against your will, without a magistrate's order.

Search your house or other premises without a magistrate's warrant, which you are entitled to see.

18 Finally

If you believe that the police are exceeding their powers in any way, you should make a note of the numbers of the officers concerned. Remember that the police should allow you to contact a lawyer 'at any stage of an investigation' provided your doing so will not cause 'unreasonable delay or hindrance to the processes of investigation or the administration of justice', and that they cannot force you to answer any questions or to sign anything.

DISCUSSION POINTS

1   'The police are doing a good job. Criticisms only make their task more difficult.' Discuss.

2   What do you think of the recently expressed view that everyone should carry an identity card bearing a set of fingerprints? This, it has been argued, would help the police enormously in tracing missing persons, indentifying bodies and tracking down suspects.

3   Do you think the police in Britain should be armed?

4   Do you think the police should be able to arrest people without a warrant?

5   It has recently been argued that no one should be questioned by the police without a magistrate being present to ensure that undue pressure is not put on suspects. What do you think?

6   Discuss the view that foreigners in Britain should not enjoy the same right as British subjects when it comes to being arrested.

7   What do you think of the idea that every citizen in Britain should be sent a copy of *Arrest* by the government free of charge?

8   'It is an infringement of a citizen's liberty for a policeman to be allowed to search his pockets.' Do you agree?

9   Ought a member of the public to assist a policeman whom he sees having difficulty with a suspect or should he mind his own business and not interfere?

10   The National Council for Civil Liberties would like the police to permit them to reproduce a photograph of a genuine warrant card in *Arrest*. The police have so far refused. Do you think this is reasonable or not?

Colin MacInnes
Nicked

from *New Society*, September 16th, 1965

This account of his own arrest by the journalist Colin MacInnes expresses many of the fears which people have about the possible abuse of their powers by the police. It is well worth remembering, however, that the police have an exceedingly difficult job to do and that compared with forces in other countries the British police have a reputation for enforcing the law with more than usual patience and tolerance.

This is what can happen when you get arrested.

Ten years ago, in the days when casinos were illegal, I went to a squalid gambling house in the East End. You reached it up a clanking metal stair, and there were two rooms, one serving food and with people sleeping for the night upon the floor, and another – separated by a grubby hanging blanket – where the card games were played. I was standing by the fire taking in this scene when six CID officers raided the place.

These were not local lads, but gentlemen from the Yard. They took us all into custody – and even roped in someone who was entering from the street as we were leaving. At the local nick they had us in one by one to interrogate us. I was somewhat alarmed to see the man who went in before me come out crying; the more so as Negroes do not often cry.

When my turn came, the detective-inspector called out 'You!' To which I answered something cheeky like 'I've got a name, you know'.

He waited till I was ahead of him, then slugged me from behind in the neck, so that I fell spreadeagled into the interrogation room.

They wanted to fingerprint me. I refused to be fingerprinted. (You can – technically – refuse this until they have a magistrate's order.) On a sign from the inspector, two of them took me into a separate room, said 'So you're not going to co-operate – huh?' and beat me around a bit. I said, 'Stop behaving like in Yankee films' – and they hit me some more.

Then I was handed over to a nice elderly chap who reasoned with me and gave me a fag. Why be so awkward? – why refuse to be printed? They could do that anyway when they got me down to Brixton, he said. I accepted the fag, but still refused the printing. About two hours later I and the dozen others were hustled off to jail – after I'd also refused to sign blind for the articles they said they'd taken from me. (I got the impression, by the way, that the local lads at the police station didn't terribly care for the way the Yard CID were handling things.)

I had not, incidentally, been charged (though no doubt a charge sheet was made out), nor had I at any time been cautioned. So two more myths about Judge's Rules (the third being the non-use of violence) turned out – as I'd always expected – to be myths indeed.

On Monday we came up before the magistrate and learned we were *all* being charged with being in possession of dangerous drugs. These alleged drugs were not produced, for at this stage they only asked for a remand and did not oppose bail. In my own case they requested from the magistrate that I should be fingerprinted. He put it to me that I couldn't possibly object to this (rather as the sergeant-major says, 'You don't mind going on fatigues, son, do you?'), so I accepted. The detective-inspector did the job. 'I was a bit surprised,' he said to me, 'by that lad who cried. He really did seem upset.' 'Well,' I answered, 'you were a bit energetic, weren't you?'

As to whether anyone *was* in possession of dangerous drugs, I simply don't know for sure. I know I hadn't any myself – and the reader can believe this or not as he pleases. I should imagine *some* were – it was that kind of a place – but I think it most unlikely that those who were dossing down on the floor for free had anything. Anyway, everyone denied it, and they stuck to this during the three times we came up (after another remand) before the magistrate.

I had meanwhile, somewhat naturally, sought advice from various sources. It was suggested to me that a bribe might help to get the charge, if not dropped, not pressed, but as I refused this contact's offer to do the necessary I cannot vouch for its possibility: all I can say is that it was proposed seriously by a knowledgeable and non-criminal person. My other advisers said I should certainly ask for trial by a judge and jury, since magistrates would always accept police evidence – so I elected (thank heaven!) to do this, even though it cost hundreds of pounds and meant waiting for months.

The reader may be wondering why I did not heroically denounce the police for their behaviour. I was advised that to do this would be to lose the case, since no one would believe me, and I would antagonize judge and jury. The thing to do, I was told, was to suggest there had been an honest error on the Law's part. So this is what I did, and I am ashamed to this day I did not have the guts to say what really happened.

Too little homework

The packet of drugs and loaded cigarette I was supposed to have, I didn't see until the third appearance in the magistrate's court. Where these came from I do not know, but I have a fair idea, and I expect the reader – if not too credulous – has as well. I did ask my lawyer, 'Look, if I'm supposed to have had those things, wouldn't my fingerprints be on them? And as they aren't can't we ask to have them examined?' Silly boy, he told me: they'll simply say that having *seen* you hold them there was no need to check them for prints, and that since my arrest they have of course been handled by dozens of official people.

In due course I appeared at the Sessions and was acquitted. The reason was simply that the police hadn't done their homework. So that when they were asked what I was supposed to have said, or where I was standing, or what I had on – simple questions of that kind to two officers (the second of whom was not allowed to hear what the first one had said in court before giving testimony himself) – they contradicted themselves. And owing to the fact that ten of the accused had already been convicted (in the magistrates' court), and the one other who could afford a lawyer had gone before a different tribunal, I had the advantage of appearing before the judge and jury alone. No doubt a collar and tie and an adequate accent were also a help.

If the reader might imagine I am still seething with indignation, or that this experience made me a copper hater, he would be quite mistaken. For what I have always (in essays and fiction) tried to establish about police work is that in certain cases, to get convictions, the police *must* use violence, perjury, and even be open to corruption. Those whom I blame are the public who will not accept this, especially when they sit on juries; or lawyers who through naïvety or a mistaken sense of public policy either accept these occurrences as normal, or refuse utterly to believe them.

The police very rarely bring a charge without grounds, simply through malice. But when they *do* bring a charge they are not over-scrupulous on how they make it stick – nor can they afford to be, with public and official pressures on them to get convictions. Nor, in this case, did I detect any *personal* animosity – I had a little chat after it with the two officers who testified against me, and they were quite amiable about losing; nor have they made things specially awkward for me since. And as they quite rightly pointed out, if you go to a dodgy place like an illegal gambling house on a Saturday night, you can easily involve yourself in – to say the least of it – misunderstandings.

I do have, however, four reproaches to make to this excellent detective-inspector and detective-constable. The first is, I don't think they should have swung this charge on me merely through guesswork. If a search revealed I had nothing, I think they might have let it go at that.

My next grouse is that I don't think they need have been quite so rough. And my next that they made no attempt whatever to find out who I was – or indeed ask me anything but my name and address and to be fingerprinted. I don't of course mean that because I am 'educated' I was entitled to favoured treatment, but I do think if they'd asked me a question or two they might have had second thoughts.

My last reproach – not my business, really – is a professional one. When they went into court they should have dovetailed their stories better. As it was, cross-examination made their tales less and less credible.

I must confess I don't like policemen as a category much, yet they do have qualities that I admire. I think they are brave (they have to be) and dedicated, and as human persons they are often fascinating. (I suppose anyone who moves in muddy moral waters must be.) The people I don't much care for are those who still believe in the Dixon of Dock Green image; this is just so silly and, factually speaking, dishonest.

As for the gentle reader of my story, I imagine his reactions thus. If he is of the respectable, he will take me for either a liar or one who seeks to rock the foundations of society. If a criminal, he will say, 'Why on earth is he making such a fuss about the obvious?' If a lawyer, he will probably think these things are best not written of. If the reader be simply one without direct experience, and seeking after facts, my strongest advice to him, so far as the Law is concerned, is to steer clear of it if possible and, if he falls into its clutches, be patient, brave and prudent.

DISCUSSION POINTS

1 'The author and the people he writes about have only themselves to blame for what occurred; they should not go to gambling houses.' Discuss.

2 Do you think that articles like *Nicked* should be printed or do you think they have the effect of bringing the police into disrepute?

3 It is thought by some people that drug-taking is such a social evil that the police should have complete powers of search and arrest in these cases and that the Judges' Rules protecting the rights of individual citizens should be disregarded. Do you agree?

4 In recent years some people whose houses have been used for drug-taking without their knowledge have been arrested, charged, convicted and sent to jail. Do you think this is just?

5 What do you think of the argument that magistrates should be specially trained people chosen from *all* sections of society and not just amateurs from the middle- and upper-classes invited to serve on the bench?

6 It could be argued that if the author had been more co-operative and less cheeky he would not have been so roughly treated. Do you agree?

7 Should prisons be places where criminals are punished or where attempts are made to reform them?

8 Should so-called 'soft' drugs be legalized?

PROJECT

Visit a magistrates' court or higher court trying criminal cases. Ask yourself in what ways the public interest is threatened by the alleged offences and what measures are employed by the courts to protect the interests of the accused.

READING

The Police, Ben Whitaker (Penguin, 1964). The problems, standards, efficiency, work, life and future of the British police force examined by an impartial observer.

Handbook of Citizens Rights, National Council for Civil Liberties. The rights of British citizens listed and explained clearly and concisely.

The following books also consider some of the problems raised in the above discussion points.

Freedom, the Individual and the Law, H. Street (Penguin, 1967).

Keeping the Peace, D. Williams (Hutchinson, 1967).

The Police and Civil Liberties, S. Bowes (Lawrence & Wishart, 1966).

Douglas Hyde
The Pope and the pill

That people should be free to make their own decisions is something that an increasing number of people in the Western world seem to be taking for granted. This was not always the case. In the past most people were happy to let strong leaders – kings, bishops, Popes – make these decisions for them. The power of monarchs and clergymen to make moral decisions for others has largely declined, but there are still many people in the world who look for guidance to individuals they regard as possessing exceptional wisdom on moral matters. This is the way most Roman Catholics regard the Pope. However, even the Pope's authority has been called into question among Catholics as a result of his pronouncement in July 1968 on the morality of birth-control. In the passage that follows, Douglas Hyde, a leading Catholic layman, discusses the 'crisis of conscience' to which the Pope's pronouncement has given rise.

Two crises – a crisis of authority and a crisis of conscience – were precipitated in the Catholic Church when, in July 1968, Pope Paul VI issued his long awaited encyclical 'Humanae Vitae'. The subject matter of the encyclical is, as the name implies, human life and, more particularly, married love. Its defence of the institution and sanctity of marriage was generally welcomed by Christians and many others besides.

The controversial section of the encyclical dealt with the Church's attitude to the morality, or immorality, of artificial methods of birth control.

Catholic thinking on the subject had taken a notable step forward when the bishops of the whole world attending the Second Vatican Council, October 1962–December 1964, recognized that family planning was legitimate and, in appropriate circumstances, desirable. It was, therefore, the means, not the end, of birth control which was up for questioning. Considerable discussion had preceded Pope Paul's encyclical, much of it turning on whether the contraceptive pill might be seen as an acceptable method. It was generally agreed that scientific development and a growing understanding of the whole psychology and physiology of sex demanded a re-examination of traditional attitudes and, if necessary, a development in the Church's teaching.

By the time Pope Paul made his pronouncement many Catholics were already using the pill in the firm belief that this was in accord with the demands of harmonious marriage and responsible parenthood. When the encyclical came it condemned outright all 'artificial' contraceptive methods including, of course, the pill.

A Church which has been known for its unity and discipline was split almost overnight into conflicting groups, for and against the encyclical. A division of opinion such as this would not in most organizations necessarily create a crisis. But the nature and traditions of the Catholic Church are such that this was described by the responsible London *Tablet* as the Church's 'darkest hour in modern history'.

The great debate started by the encyclical quickly began to turn, not just on the means by which family planning might legitimately be achieved but upon the nature and extent of Papal authority and of authority generally within the Church. Equally explosive in its implications was the related discussion on the Church's attitude to the conscience of the individual Catholic who finds himself unable to accept some aspects of its teaching. Primacy of conscience has been an accepted part of traditional Catholic belief. But just what did this mean in circumstances like these?

The clergy were directly affected in their role as teachers, counsellors and confessors though not, since they are celibates, in the same intimate way as the married laity. Even so, this was sufficient to create a crisis of conscience for many including theologians of international repute as well as ordinary priests engaged in pastoral work. In dioceses where there were hard-line bishops, notably in Southwark, England, and Washington, DC, USA, some were suspended, others silenced. The general consensus among bishops, however, seemed to be that a far greater latitude than is normal should be permitted those who had difficulty in accepting the Pope's teaching.

In his encyclical, Pope Paul accepts as admissible the 'rhythm' method of birth control based upon the so-called 'safe' or infertile, period, but condemns 'every action which, either in anticipation of the conjugal act, or in its accomplishment, or in the development of its consequences, proposes, whether as an end or as a means, to render procreation impossible'.

'Each exercise of the marriage act,' says the encyclical, 'must remain in itself open to the transmission of life.' Intercourse during infertile periods does not destroy the act's openness to the transmission of life, and is therefore permissible. This distinction was publicly challenged as unreal by numerous priests and laymen.

The 'rhythm' method, which received the Papal blessing, is in any case generally thought to be unsatisfactory, the least reliable and the most difficult for uneducated people to understand and practise.

Pope Paul appealed to the traditional teaching of the Christian Church, the natural law, and what he described as the 'biological processes'. Critics were quick to point out that the encyclical had relied very little on theological arguments despite the fact that it was reasonable to suppose that it would be from this that he, as Pope, could reason with the greatest authority. The weakness of the appeal to tradition, said the critics, was that there is for practical purposes no long tradition of thought on this question since artificial birth control – coitus interruptus apart – was virtually unknown until modern times. Moreover there has been a very considerable development in Catholic teaching on the approach to the marriage act in recent years. For example, Pope Pius XII and still more the Second Vatican Council, acknowledged the fruitful role that it can play in cementing in love the partnership of husband and wife. This is in marked contrast to the approach of St Jerome, St Ambrose and St Augustine whose view of sex as something inherently shameful dominated the Church's teaching for many centuries.

The Pope was on even weaker ground, the dissenters asserted, when he appealed to natural law, by which is meant that there is a certain, fixed, unchanging code of conduct which man instinctively and through his reason can recognize as right. Yet a purely rational approach by modern men to modern problems would seem to lead to acceptance of contraception rather than to its rejection. Such evidence as there is of the practices of primitive peoples living in a 'natural' state is, put at its highest, inconclusive. And, having called in a wide range of advisers, and taken four years to make up his mind on the question, Pope Paul had himself demonstrated that it was possible to entertain the idea of a change in the 'unchanging' pattern of the natural law.

So far as the 'biological' argument went, he had rejected the opinion of lay experts, doctors, gynaecologists, married couples, whom he had appointed to a commission charged with a study of the question and who had practically unanimously come down on the side of the use of artificial contraception.

That the encyclical should have its critics was to be expected. What was unusual and of exceptional significance was that the most outspoken and carefully reasoned criticism came from within the Church itself, and not from some irresponsible fringe but from much respected priests, laymen and Catholic journals many of whom could not possibly be described as *avant garde*. In recent years educated laymen have been increasingly drawn into the life and activity of the Church. It was notable that these were amongst the most active and outspoken of the encyclical's critics.

Given the hierarchical structure of the Church and a tradition of unquestioning obedience to superiors the wave of criticism which swept through its ranks amounted in itself to a challenge to authority. But the challenge became more specific than this for the debate quickly and, once it had started, almost inevitably, moved on from the discussion of 'Humanae Vitae' to the whole question of authority in the Church. It was not only what the Pope had done that was questioned but the way he had done it.

It had originally been intended that the First Vatican Council which met in Rome 1869–70 should spell out the whole nature and structure of the Church, including just where authority lay and how it was exercised. The Council, however, had got no further than defining the Pope's authority – with the well known emphasis upon Papal primacy and infallibility – when it was brought to an abrupt end by the invasion of the Papal States by the Piedmontese armies. This left the Church in a position where, according to some friendly critics, it was not unlike an absolute monarchy. Vatican II, called together by Pope John XXIII, ninety-two years later, resumed the discussion. Its Dogmatic Constitution on the Church, which is the document that deals with the Church's authority, has been hailed as its most momentous achievement. In it the bishops are seen as constituting a 'college' with collective responsibility for the tasks of the entire Church. More, the document declared that 'the body of the faithful as a whole . . . cannot err in matters of belief. Thanks to a supernatural sense of the Faith which characterizes the People as a whole, it manifests this unerring quality when, from the bishops down to the last member of the laity, it shows universal agreement in matters of faith and morals'.

Thus authority was seen as something which could extend to all those who make up the Church, the Pope, the 'college' of bishops and the whole of the faithful. It particularly emphasized the collegiality of the bishops. Because of the spread of education, the documents of the Second Vatican Council have been far more widely discussed by priests and laymen alike than those of any previous Council and so the Pope's verdict on birth control was awaited with additional interest. Would Paul invoke the principle of collegiality by directly associating the bishops with his enquiries and his decisions? Would he aim at a consensus by listening to the views of the faithful? In practice, he ignored the collegiality of the bishops, taking the matter out of the hands of the Council and making the decision exclusively his own. He ignored the opinions of a majority of those theologians and of all the lay people whom he had brought in as advisers. Subsequent events suggested that by thus asserting the primacy of the Papacy he at the same time weakened it. In the new openness and questioning encouraged by the Council itself, there were priests and laymen who expressed the fear that he was still clinging to the old concept of the 'absolute monarchy' and so had not acted in accord with the spirit of the Council.

It can be argued that Pope Paul himself truly reflects his Church's situation at this moment since in it two warring, schizophrenic trends, the traditional and the modern, are to be seen, just as they are so visibly embodied in the one very complex man. Be that as it may, a significant thing about the discussion on authority was that those who voiced their criticisms either individually or, as also happened, in groups, or who made known their intentions to ignore the Papal ruling, were clearly in good conscience. So to the crisis of authority was added one of conscience. This in time led on to a discussion of the very nature of conscience itself.

First the Belgian, then the German and in due course the English hierarchy acknowledged that the primacy of conscience was a traditional teaching which the Church both advocated and respected. Said the Belgian bishops: 'Someone who is competent in the matter under consideration and capable of forming a personal and well-founded judgement – which necessarily presupposed a sufficient amount of knowledge – may, after a serious examination before God, come to other conclusions on certain points. In such a case he has the right to follow his conviction provided that he remains sincerely disposed to continue his enquiry.'

It will be noted that whilst the primacy of conscience was asserted it was also qualified.

The bishops of England and Wales, in a joint statement addressed to their people, declared that: 'Neither this Encyclical nor any other document of the Church takes away from us our right and duty to follow our conscience.' They went on to recall that the Second Vatican Council had said that 'In the formation of their consciences the Christian faithful ought carefully to attend to the sacred and certain doctrine of the Church.'

The emphasis on conscience was, therefore, not as unambiguous a lead to those whose reason refused to accept the Pope's arguments as might appear. Catholics are taught that for them conscience must be informed by the Church – by means of Papal and episcopal utterances, by pulpit homilies and by Catholic education. To non-Catholics, in particular, it looked as though the Church was now trying to have it both ways. The Council had provided a welcome new emphasis when it stressed the primacy of conscience but, when the test came, ecclesiastical authority said: 'Ah, yes, you must follow the dictates of conscience but the one you follow must be that formed by the Church. If you take any other course you are in bad conscience.' In practice, most bishops seemed to accept that in the final analysis conscience, whatever its dictates, should be followed. But, it was stressed, conscience can be a subjective and unreliable thing. For this reason it needs to be both formed and informed.

Pope Paul had not sought a consensus of the faithful before issuing his encyclical. The effect of its publication was to launch such a deep-probing discussion that a consensus could conceivably be arrived at after the event, although few would suppose that this would be accepted in Paul's lifetime. It certainly increased the likelihood of the future collaboration of the whole of the 'Peoples of God' – all the faithful, Pope, bishops, lay people – in the making of decisions. This would be in accord with the earliest Christian traditions, for descriptions of early

Douglas Hyde

Councils suggest that they may have come nearer to 'participatory democracy' than anything the Church has known in modern times.

DISCUSSION POINTS

1 Can any one person, however exalted, have a monopoly of the truth?

2 What do you think of the argument that since sexual intercourse is for the purpose of reproduction, engaging in it simply for pleasure is an abuse and therefore immoral?

3 Who is more admirable – the man who accepts the authority of 'those who know better than him', or the man who makes every effort to find out the facts for himself and solve his own problems?

4 It is often argued that there is fundamentally no difference between the 'rhythm' method (approved of by the Roman Catholic Church) and any other contraceptive techniques – they are all calculated ways of preventing pregnancy. The only difference is that the 'rhythm' method is particularly unreliable. What do you think?

5 Should a person act in accordance with his own conscience or in accordance with the commands of those who 'know better than him'?

6 What do you think of the view that if something is the truth it is true for all time and so the Church cannot change its view without admitting that it was wrong in the past?

7 Does the use of contraception violate the 'law of nature'?

8 'The Pope was right to ignore the advice of the medical experts he had asked to study this question; after all it is a moral problem which they have no authority to pronounce upon.' Discuss.

9 Is it right that priests who publicly disagree with the Pope over birth-control should be removed from their posts?

10 Is tradition always a barrier to progress and individual liberty?

PROJECTS

Compare the way the Roman Catholic Church and the Communist Party deals with heretics. A further comparison could be made of methods employed against intellectuals by some 'democratic' govern-ments – e.g. South Africa, the USA.

READING

I Believed Douglas Hyde (Pan Books, 1947). The autobiography of a journalist who left the Communist Party and joined the Roman Catholic Church.

Years Off My Life, A. V. Gorbatov (Constable, 1964). A Soviet General's experiences of the Stalin purges.

Ward 7, Valeriy Tarsis (Collins and Harvill Press, 1965). An account of life in a Soviet mental home for the sane.

The Spanish Inquisition, Henry Kamen (Weidenfeld, 1965). A history of the persecution of intellectuals by the Roman Catholic Church.

117 Days, Ruth First (Penguin, 1965). An account of confinement and interrogation under the South African Ninety-Day Detention Law.

James Baldwin
Growing up in the Deep South

from *The Fire Next Time*, Michael Joseph, 1963

In some societies a man's colour or racial origins may make him an object of prejudice and discrimination, so that his freedom to live as others do is greatly restricted. James Baldwin, an American Negro, has written a great deal about the situation of the black man in the United States. In the following passage from *The Fire Next Time*, Baldwin tells of his early conversion to Christianity, in the past one of the only outlets for ambition and creative drive available to the Negro in America.

As I look back, everything I did seems curiously deliberate, though it certainly did not seem deliberate then. For example, I did not join the church of which my father was a member and in which he preached. My best friend in school, who attended a different church, had already 'surrendered his life to the Lord', and he was very anxious about my soul's salvation. (I wasn't, but any human attention was better than none.) One Saturday afternoon, he took me to his church. There were no services that day, and the church was empty, except for some women cleaning and some other women praying. My friend took me into the back room to meet his pastor – a woman. There she sat, in her robes, smiling, an extremely proud and handsome woman, with Africa, Europe, and the America of the American Indian blended in her face. She was perhaps forty-five or fifty at this time, and in our world she was a very celebrated woman. My friend was about to introduce me when she looked at me and smiled and said, 'Whose little boy are you?'

Now this, unbelievably, was precisely the phrase used by pimps and racketeers on the Avenue when they suggested, both humorously and intensely, that I 'hang out' with them. Perhaps part of the terror they had caused me to feel came from the fact that I unquestionably wanted to be *somebody's* little boy. I was so frightened, and at the mercy of so many conundrums, that inevitably, that summer, *someone* would have taken me over; one doesn't, in Harlem, long remain standing on any auction block. It was my good luck – perhaps – that I found myself in the church racket instead of some other, and surrendered to a spiritual seduction long before I came to any carnal knowledge. For when the pastor asked me, with that marvellous smile, 'Whose little boy are you?' my heart replied at once, 'Why, yours.'

The summer wore on, and things got worse. I became more guilty and more frightened, and kept all this bottled up inside me, and naturally, inescapably, one night, when this woman had finished preaching, everything came roaring, screaming, crying out, and I fell to the ground before the altar. It was the strangest sensation I have ever had in my life – up to that time, or since. I had not known that it was going to happen, or that it could happen. One moment I was on my feet, singing and clapping and, at the same time, working out in my head the plot of a play I was working on then; the next moment, with no transition, no sensation of falling, I was on my back, with the lights beating down into my face and all the vertical saints above me. I did not know what I was doing down so low, or how I had got there. And the anguish that filled me cannot be described. It moved in me like one of those floods that devastate counties, tearing everything down, tearing children from their parents and lovers from each other, and making everything an unrecognizable waste. All I really remember is the pain, the unspeakable pain; it was as though I were yelling up to Heaven and Heaven would not hear me. And if Heaven would not hear me, if love could not descend from Heaven – to wash me, to make me clean – then utter disaster was my portion. Yes, it does indeed mean something – something unspeakable – to be born, in a white country, an Anglo-Teutonic, antisexual country, black. You very soon, without knowing it, give up all hope of communion. Black people, mainly, look down or look up but do not look at each other, not at you, and white people, mainly, look away. And the universe is simply a sounding drum; there is no way, no way whatever, so it seemed then and has sometimes seemed since, to get through a life, to love your wife and children, or your friends, or your mother and father, or to be loved. The universe, which is not merely the stars and the moon and the planets, flowers, grass, and trees, but *other people*, has evolved no terms for your existence, has made no room for you, and if love will not swing wide the gates, no other power will or can. And if one despairs – as who has not? – of human love, God's love alone is left. But God – and I felt this even then, so long ago, on that tremendous floor, unwillingly – is white. And if His love was so great, and if He loved all His children, why were we, the blacks, cast down so far? Why? In spite of all I said thereafter, I found no answer on the floor – not *that* answer, anyway – and I was on the floor all night. Over me, to bring me 'through', the saints sang and rejoiced and prayed. And in the morning, when they raised me, they told me that I was 'saved'.

Well, indeed I was, in a way, for I was utterly drained and exhausted and released, for the first time, from all my guilty torment. I was aware then only of my relief. For many years, I could not ask myself why human relief had to be achieved in a fashion at once so pagan and so desperate – in a fashion at once so unspeakably old and so unutterably new. And by the time I was able to ask myself this question, I was also able to see that the principles governing the rites and customs of the churches in which I grew up did not differ from the principles governing the rites and customs of other churches, white. The principles were Blindness, Loneliness, and Terror, the first principle necessarily and actively cultivated in order to deny the two others. I would love to believe that the principles were Faith, Hope, and Charity, but this is clearly not so for most Christians, or for what we call the Christian world.

I was saved. But at the same time, out of a deep, adolescent cunning I do not pretend to understand, I realized immediately that I could not remain in the church merely as another worshipper. I would have to give myself something to do, in order not to be too bored and find myself among all the wretched unsaved of the Avenue. And I don't doubt that I also intended to best my father on his own ground. Anyway, very shortly after I joined the church, I became a preacher – a Young Minister – and I remained in the pulpit for more than three years. My youth quickly made me a much bigger drawing card than my father. I pushed this advantage ruthlessly, for it was the most effective means I had found of breaking his hold over me. That was the most frightening time of my life, and quite the most dishonest, and the resulting hysteria lent great passion to my sermons – for a while. I relished the attention and the relative immunity from punishment that my new status gave me, and I relished, above all, the sudden right to privacy. It had to be recognized, after all, that I was still a schoolboy, with my schoolwork to do, and I was also expected to prepare at least one sermon a week. During what we may call my heyday, I preached much more often than that. This meant that there were hours and even whole days when I could not be interrupted – not even by my father. I had immobilized him. It took rather more time for me to realize that I had also immobilized myself, and had escaped from nothing whatever.

The church was very exciting. It took a long time for me to disengage myself from this excitement, and on the blindest, most visceral level, I never really have, and never will. There is no music like that music, no drama like the drama of the saints rejoicing, the sinners moaning, the tambourines racing, and all those voices coming together and crying holy unto the Lord. There is still, for me, no pathos quite like the pathos of those multi-coloured, worn, somehow triumphant and transfigured faces, speaking from the depths of a visible, tangible, continuing despair of the goodness of the Lord. I have never seen anything to equal the fire and excitement that sometimes, without warning, fill a church, causing the church, as Leadbelly and so many others have testified, to 'rock'. Nothing that has happened to me since equals the power and the glory that I sometimes felt when, in the middle of a sermon, I knew that I was somehow, by some miracle, really carrying, as they said, 'the Word' – when the church and I were one. Their pain and their joy were mine, and mine were theirs – they surrendered their pain and joy to me, I surrendered mine to them – and their cries of 'Amen!' and 'Hallelujah!' and 'Yes, Lord!' and 'Praise His name!' and 'Preach it, brother!' sustained and whipped on my solos until we all became equal, wringing wet, singing and dancing, in anguish and rejoicing, at the foot of the altar. It was, for a long time, in spite of – or, not inconceivably, because of – the shabbiness of my motives, my only sustenance, my meat and drink. I rushed home from school, to the church, to the altar, to be alone there, to commune with Jesus, my dearest Friend, who would never fail me, who knew all the secrets of my heart. Perhaps He did, but I didn't, and the bargain we struck, actually, down there at the foot of the cross, was that He would never let me find out.

He failed His bargain. He was a much better Man than I took Him for. It happened, as things do, imperceptibly, in many ways at once. I date it – the slow crumbling of my faith, the pulverization of my fortress – from the time, about a year after I had begun to preach, when I began to read again. I justified this desire by the fact that I was still in school, and I began, fatally, with Dostoyevsky. By this time, I was in a high school that was predominantly Jewish. This meant that I was surrounded by people who were, by definition, beyond any hope of salvation, who laughed at the tracts and leaflets I brought to school, and who pointed out that the Gospels had been written long after the death of Christ. This might not have been so distressing if it had not forced me to read the tracts and leaflets myself, for they were indeed, unless one believed their message already, impossible to believe. I remember feeling dimly that there was a kind of blackmail in it. People, I felt, ought to love the Lord *because* they loved Him. and not because they were afraid of going to Hell. I was forced, reluctantly, to realize that the Bible itself had been written by men, and translated by men out of languages I could not read, and I was already, without quite admitting it to myself, terribly involved with the effort of putting words on paper. Of course, I had the rebuttal ready: These men had all been operating under divine inspiration. *Had* they? *All* of them? And I also knew by now, alas, far more about divine inspiration than I dared admit, for I knew how I worked myself up into my own visions and how frequently – indeed, incessantly – the visions God granted to me differed from the visions He granted to my father. I did not understand the dreams I had at night, but I knew that they were not holy. For that matter, I knew that my waking hours were far from holy. I spent most of my time in a state of repentance for things I had vividly desired to do but had not done. The fact that I was dealing with Jews brought the whole question of colour, which I had been desperately avoiding, into the terrified centre of my mind. I realized that the Bible had been written by white men. I knew that, according to many Christians, I was a descendant of Ham, who had been cursed, and that I was therefore predestined to be a slave. This had nothing to do with anything I was, or contained, or could become; my fate had been sealed for ever, from the beginning of time. And it seemed, indeed, when one looked out over Christendom, that this was what Christendom effectively believed. It was certainly the way it behaved. I remembered the Italian priests and bishops blessing Italian boys who were on their way to Ethiopia.

Again, the Jewish boys in high school were troubling because I could find no point of connection between them and the Jewish pawn-brokers and landlords and grocery-store owners in Harlem. I knew that these people were Jews – God knows I was told it often enough – but I though of them only as white. Jews, as such, until I got to high school, were all incarcerated in the Old Testament, and their names were

Abraham, Moses, Daniel, Ezekiel, and Job, and Shadrach, Meshach, and Abednego. It was bewildering to find them so many miles and centuries out of Egypt, and so far from the fiery furnace. My best friend in high school was a Jew. He came to our house once, and afterwards my father asked, as he asked about everyone, 'is he a Christian?' – by which he meant 'Is he saved?' I really do not know whether my answer came out of innocence or venom, but I said coldly, 'No. He's Jewish.' My father slammed me across the face with his great palm, and in that moment everything flooded back – all the hatred and all the fear, and the depth of a merciless resolve to kill my father rather than allow my father to kill me – and I knew that all those sermons and tears and all that repentance and rejoicing had changed nothing. I wondered if I was expected to be glad that a friend of mine, or anyone, was to be tormented for ever in Hell, and I also thought, suddenly, of the Jews in another Christian nation, Germany. They were not so far from the fiery furnace after all, and my best friend might have been one of them. I told my father, 'He's a better Christian than you are,' and walked out of the house. The battle between us was in the open, but that was all right; it was almost a relief. A more deadly struggle had begun.

Being in the pulpit was like being in the theatre; I was behind the scenes and knew how the illusion was worked. I knew the other ministers and knew the quality of their lives. And I don't mean to suggest by this the 'Elmer Gantry' sort of hypocrisy concerning sensuality; it was a deeper, deadlier, and more subtle hypocrisy than that, and a little honest sensuality, or a lot, would have been like water in an extremely bitter desert. I knew how to work on a congregation until the last dime was surrendered – it was not very hard to do – and I knew where the money for 'the Lord's work' went. I knew, though I did not wish to know it, that I had no respect for the people with whom I worked. I could not have said it then, but I also knew that if I continued I would soon have no respect for myself. And the fact that I was 'the young Brother Baldwin' increased my value with those same pimps and racketeers who had helped to stampede me into the church in the first place. They still saw the little boy they intended to take over. They were waiting for me to come to my senses and realize that I was in a very lucrative business. They knew that I did not yet realize this, and also that I had not yet begun to suspect where my own needs, *coming up* (they were very patient), could drive me. They themselves did know the score, and they knew that the odds were in their favour. And, really, I knew it, too. I was even lonelier and more vulnerable than I had been before. And the blood of the Lamb had not cleansed me in any way whatever. I was just as black as I had been the day that I was born. Therefore, when I faced a congregation, it began to take all the strength I had not to stammer, not to curse, not to tell them to throw away their Bibles and get off their knees and go home and organize, for example, a rent strike. When I watched all the children, their copper, brown, and beige faces staring up at me as I taught Sunday school, I felt that I was committing a crime in talking about the gentle Jesus, in telling them to reconcile themselves to their misery on earth in order to gain the crown of eternal life. Were only Negroes to gain this crown? Was Heaven, then, to be merely another ghetto? Perhaps I might have been able to reconcile myself even to this if I had been able to believe that there was any loving kindness to be found in the haven I represented. But I had been in the pulpit too long and I had seen too many monstrous things. I don't refer merely to the glaring fact that the minister eventually acquires houses and Cadillacs while the faithful continue to scrub floors and drop their dimes and quarters and dollars into the plate. I really mean that there was no love in the church. It was a mask for hatred and self-hatred and despair. The transfiguring power of the Holy Ghost ended when the service ended, and salvation stopped at the church door. When we were told to love everybody, I had thought that that meant *everybody*. But no. It applied only to those who believed as we did, and it did not apply to white people at all. I was told by a minister, for example, that I should never, on any public conveyance, under any circumstances, rise and give my seat to a white woman. White men never rose for Negro women. Well, that was true enough, in the main – I saw his point. But what was the point, the purpose, of *my* salvation if it did not permit me to behave with love towards others, no matter how they behaved towards me? What others did was their responsibility, for which they would answer when the judgement trumpet sounded. But what *I* did was *my* responsibility, and I would have to answer, too – unless, of course, there was also in Heaven a special dispensation for the benighted black, who was not to be judged in the same way as other human beings, or angels. It probably occurred to me around this time that the vision people hold of the world to come is but a reflection, with predictable wishful distortions, of the world in which they live. And this did not apply only to Negroes, who were no more 'simple' or 'spontaneous' or 'Christian' than anybody else – who were merely more oppressed. In the same way that we, for white people, were the descendants of Ham, and were cursed for ever, white people were, for us, the descendants of Cain. And the passion with which we loved the Lord was a measure of how deeply we feared and distrusted and, in the end, hated almost all strangers, always, and avoided and despised outselves.

But I cannot leave it at that; there is more to it than that. In spite of everything, there was in the life I led a zest and a joy and a capacity for facing and surviving disaster that are very moving and very rare. Perhaps we were, all of us – pimps, whores, racketeers, church members, and children – bound together by the nature of our oppression, the specific and peculiar complex of risks we had to run; if so, within these limits we sometimes achieved with each other a freedom that was close to love. I remember, anyway, church suppers and outings, and, later, after I left the church, rent and waistline parties where rage and sorrow sat in the darkness and did not stir, and we ate and drank and talked and laughed and danced and forgot all about 'the man'. We had the liquor, the chicken, the music, and each other, and had no need to pretend to be what we were not. This is the freedom that one hears in some gospel songs, for example, and in jazz. In all jazz, and especially in the blues, there is something tart and ironic, authoritative and double-edged. White Americans seem to feel that happy songs are *happy* and sad songs are *sad*, and that, God help us, is exactly the way most white Americans sing them – sounding, in both cases, so helplessly, defencelessly fatuous that one dare not speculate on the temperature of the deep freeze from which issue their brave and sexless little voices. Only people who have been 'down the line', as the song puts it, know what this music is about, I think it was Big Bill Broonzy who used to sing 'I Feel So Good'. a really joyful song about a man who is on his way to the railroad station to meet his girl. She's coming home. It is the singer's incredibly moving exuberance that makes one realize how leaden the time must have been while she was gone. There is no guarantee that she will stay this time, either, as the singer clearly knows, and, in fact, she has not yet actually arrived. Tonight, or tomorrow, or within the next five minutes, he may very well be singing 'Lonesome in My Bedroom', or insisting, 'Ain't we, ain't we, going to make it all right? Well, if we don't today, we will tomorrow night.' White Americans do not understand the depths out of which such an ironic tenacity comes, but they suspect that the force is sensual, and they are terrified of sensuality and do not any longer understand it. The word 'sensual' is not intended to bring to mind quivering dusky maidens or priapic black studs. I am referring to something much simpler and much less fanciful.

To be sensual, I think, is to respect and rejoice in the force of life, of life itself, and to be *present* in all that one does, from the effort of loving to the breaking of bread. It will be a great day for America, incidentally, when we begin to eat bread again, instead of the blasphemous and tasteless foam rubber that we have substituted for it. And I am not being frivolous now, either. Something very sinister happens to the people of a country when they begin to distrust their own reactions as deeply as they do here, and become as joyless as they have become. It is this individual uncertainty on the part of white American men and women, this inability to renew themselves at the fountain of their own lives, that makes the discussion, let alone elucidation, of any conundrum – that is, any reality – so supremely difficult. The person who distrusts himself has no touchstone for reality – for this touchstone can be only oneself. Such a person interposes between himself and reality nothing less than a labyrinth of attitudes. And these attitudes, furthermore, though the person is usually unaware of it (is unaware of so much), are historical and public attitudes. They do not relate to the present any more than they relate to the person. Therefore, whatever white people do not know about Negroes reveals, precisely and inexorably, what they do not know about themselves.

White Christians have also forgotten several elementary historical details. They have forgotten that the religion that is now identified with their virtue and their power – 'God is on our side,' says Dr Verwoerd – came out of a rocky piece of ground in what is now known as the Middle East before colour was invented, and that in order for the Christian church to be established, Christ had to be put to death, by Rome, and that the real architect of the Christian church was not the disreputable, sun-baked Hebrew who gave it his name but the mercilessly fanatical and self-righteous St Paul. The energy that was buried with the rise of the Christian nations must come back into the world; nothing can prevent it. Many of us, I think, both long to see this happen and are terrified of it, for though this transformation contains the hope of liberation, it also imposes a necessity for great change. But in order to deal with the untapped and dormant force of the previously subjugated, in order to survive as a human, moving, moral weight in the world, America and all the Western nations will be forced to re-examine themselves and release themselves from many things that are now taken to be sacred, and to discard nearly all the assumptions that have been used to justify their lives and their anguish and their crimes so long.

'The white man's Heaven,' sings a Black Muslim minister, 'is the black man's Hell.' One may object – possibly – that this puts the matter somewhat too simply, but the song is true, and it has been true for as long as white men have ruled the world. The Africans put it another way: When the white man came to Africa, the white man had the Bible and the African had the land, but now it is the white man who is being, reluctantly and bloodily, separated from the land, and the African who is still attempting to digest or to vomit up the Bible. The struggle, therefore, that now begins in the world is extremely complex, involving the historical role of Christianity in the realm of power – that is, politics – and in the realm of morals. In the realm of power, Christianity has operated with an unmitigated arrogance and cruelty – necessarily, since a religion ordinarily imposes on those who have discovered the true faith the spiritual duty of liberating the infidels. This particular true faith, moreover, is more deeply concerned about the soul than it is about the body, to which fact the flesh (and the corpses) of countless infidels bears witness. It goes without saying, then, that whoever questions the authority of the true faith also contests the right of the nations that hold this faith to rule over him – contests, in short, their title to his land. The spreading of the Gospel, regardless of the motives or the integrity or the heroism of some of the missionaries, was an absolutely indispensable justification for the planting of the flag. Priests and nuns and school-teachers helped to protect and sanctify the power that was so ruthlessly being used by people who were indeed seeking a city, but not one in the heavens, and one to be made, very definitely, by captive hands. The Christian church itself – again, as distinguished from some of its ministers – sanctified and rejoiced in the conquests of the flag, and encouraged, if it did not formulate, the belief that conquest, with the resulting relative well-being of the Western populations, was proof of the favour of God. God had come a long way from the desert – but then so had Allah, though in a very different direction. God, going north, and rising on the wings of power, had become white, and Allah, out of power, and on the dark side of Heaven, had become – for all practical purposes, anyway – black. Thus, in the realm of morals the role of Christianity has been, at best, ambivalent. Even leaving out of account the remarkable arrogance that assumed that the ways and morals of others were inferior to those of Christians, and that they therefore had every right, and could use any means, to change them, the collision between cultures – and the schizophrenia in the mind of Christendom – had rendered the domain of morals as chartless as the sea once was, and as treacherous as the sea still is. It is not too much to say that whoever wishes to become a truly moral human being (and let us not ask whether or not this is possible; I think we must *believe* that it is possible) must first divorce himself from all the prohibitions, crimes and hypocrisies of the Christian church. If the concept of God has any validity or any use, it can only be to make us larger, freer, and more loving. If God cannot do this, then it is time we got rid of Him.

DISCUSSION POINTS

1 'An individual who undergoes a dramatic conversion to a religious or political faith in the way the author describes his own early conversion to Christianity, has become a prisoner of his emotions. His reason is now shackled by faith.' How far do you agree with this view?

2 In what ways can colour prejudice and discrimination limit the liberty of a black man in a predominantly white society?

3 Are Christianity and racialism compatible?

4 What do you think of the idea that religion is just a form of escape from the unpleasantness of the real world?

5 In recent years some churches have attempted to attract young people by introducing so-called folk masses and pop music. Is this likely to have the effect the churches want or does it simply bring them into contempt with the public?

6 Consider the view that it is a denial of man's fundamental rights to allow or insist upon deprived minority groups living in ghettoes.

PROJECT

How does the race problem in the United States of America compare with that in Britain?

READING

The Fire Next Time, James Baldwin (Penguin, 1964). The problem of race in America seen from a Negro point of view.

Autobiography, Malcolm X (Hutchinson, 1966). The story of one of the first advocates of Black Power, assassinated by a rival Negro group in 1967.

Black Like Me, J. H. Griffin (Panther, 1964). The disturbing story of a white American who, after dyeing himself black, set out to find what life was really like for the Negro in America.

Racial Discrimination in England (Penguin, 1968). A study of the extent and nature of racial discrimination in England based on the much-publicized PEP Report of 1967.

How Colour Prejudiced is Britain? Clifford Hill (Gollancz, 1965). A book whose title speaks for itself.

Jamaican Migrant, Wallace Collins (Routledge, 1965). The story of a young West Indian's experiences as an immigrant to Britain.

Back Street New Worlds, Elspeth Huxley (Chatto & Windus, 1964). Originally written as a series of articles for the magazine *Punch*, this book takes a look at the various groups of immigrants who have settled in Britain.

Facts paper on colour and immigration in the United Kingdom 1968 (Research Publications, 1968). Official figures on a question on which reliable information is scarce.

Henry Fairlie
Martin Luther King

from *Encounter*, June, 1968

The history of Negro slavery in the Deep South of America seems to have left a deep mark on relations between black and white in that country. Some whites have come to see the black man as an inferior kind of human being, a belief for which there is absolutely no scientific support. Some blacks, outraged by the indignity of their situation, have reacted with extreme violence and have come to advocate Black Power, the idea that black men should govern themselves in separate states of America. They are preaching the view that, far from being inferior to the white man, the black man is in fact innately superior. Martin Luther King, the leader of the Civil Rights movement in America, was a liberal-minded man who believed passionately that all men, whatever the colour of their skin, are potentially equal and capable of living together in harmony one day. He rejected outright the view that white and black men are a threat to each other's existence and that the only solution is the domination of one by the other or total separation. He was shot to death in 1968.

'*You can liberate a freeman, but you cannot liberate a slave.*' That is the first and the last thing to be said about Martin Luther King. Almost alone among American Negro leaders, he had ceased to be a slave. He had become a free man, who could be liberated as a human being. Almost every other American Negro leader, from the Uncle Toms to the SNCC extremists, is still bound in the wheel of slavery. Almost none can escape the memory of it. They are slaves still; and it is to slavery, like Nat Turner, that they react. Stokely Carmichael and H. Rap Brown are not yet free men. 'It is the nature of slavery,' says Louis Halle again, 'to render its victims so abject that at last, fearing to be free, they multiply their own chains.' This is the Black Power leader. He fastens fetters to himself even as he screams for freedom. Martin Luther King, almost alone, had escaped from slavery, whereas others have escaped only from the slave-owners. He had surmounted it, had left it behind, and could think and feel, act and speak, as a free man.

He was not a saint, he was a man; a whole and liberated man, while so many others, white as well as black, remained slaves. This was his greatness; and this, above all, was his prophecy.

Martin Luther King was given to America by the South. The South may have killed him – we do not know yet – but it was the South also which bore him. He himself would have made the acknowledgement. It meant everything that he was buried in a Baptist Church of the South, to the hymns of the South, to the rhetoric of the South, to the prayers of the South: the black South maybe, but still the South.

'Go gently into the South,' I was advised when I first came to America three years ago, and I took the advice. I journeyed slowly through Virginia, through North Carolina and South Carolina, until at last I reached Georgia; and there, for a time, I stopped to survey the civilization in which I had arrived, before pushing on to the dark interior of the South, in Alabama and Mississippi and Louisiana, where the civilization has survived, until now, a closed and arrested society. Like almost all who know the South, I found that I grew more and more fascinated by it: that I grew to love it and to fear it; and then to love it more and fear it more. Not the white South or the black South, but the South itself, in which, as W. J. Cash said, 'Negro entered into white man as white man entered into Negro,' the relationship between them 'nothing less than organic'. That the Negro problem in America was ceasing to be a Southern problem was one of the most directly personal difficulties which Martin Luther King encountered.

All the qualities of the South, as Cash pointed out, find expression in its fondness for rhetoric, a 'gorgeous, primitive art, addressed to the autonomic system and not to the encephalon'; and in the South, from the beginning, 'there was the daily impact upon the white man of the example of the Negro, concerning whom nothing is so certain as his remarkable tendency to seize on lovely words, to roll them in his throat, to heap them in redundant profusion one upon another until meaning vanishes and there is nothing left but the sweet, canorous drunkenness of sound.'

I first heard Southern rhetoric at an annual open-air gathering of red-neck farmers in the tidelands of Virginia. I heard it again at a Ku Klux Klan rally, at Durham in North Carolina, cross-burning preceded by hour upon hour of speeches, of primitive rhythm, of the 'canorous drunkenness of sound'. I heard it again from a sheriff, in front of a courthouse in Mississippi. But I heard it most often whenever I went to a Negro church in the South, and listened as the Biblical prose was churned into passionate oratory, flung by the preacher to his congregation in mounting cadences, until at last, all voluntary power surrendered, they flung back their *Amens* at every sentence. It is one of the sounds of the South which stay with me: the *Amens* of the white Klan rally and the black Baptist congregation, in the heaviness of the heat and the moist, impossible to tell apart, since the voice is the same, the voice of the South.

This was the instrument which Martin Luther King took from the South, translating it to his own use, until all America listened to it as its own prophecy, and even all the world listened and claimed it as its voice.

In the most famous passage of his most famous speech, before the Lincoln Memorial in Washington, in 1963, three centuries of the rhetoric of the South were pulled together into one exalted outburst. Every device ever contrived by every preacher of the South, black or white, was put to use, until his huge audience, black and white, had been carried beyond itself, no longer merely the sum of its members. He bit into the gathering *Amens*, the answering 'Yeah! Yeah!', the thundering applause, for they were not to be allowed to rest, but were to be carried to a higher pitch with each ejaculation.

It went like this.

I have a dream that one day even the State of Mississippi, a desert sweltering with the heat of injustice and oppression

'Yeah! Yeah!' –

will be transformed into an oasis of freedom and justice.

– the *Amens* roll into the rising applause. He does not let them die:

I have a dream that my four little children

– 'Amen! Amen!' 'Yeah! Yeah!'

will one day live in a nation where they will not be judged by the colour of their skin but by the content of their character

– the *Amens* and the applause swell. But he bites into them:

I have a dream today.

The applause rises, held now in anticipation of what is to come:

I have a dream that one day the State of Alabama. . . .

And so on, until he bites again into the applause, with the reiterated, 'I have a dream today,' as he carries the audience to the final:

I have a dream that one day every valley shall be exalted, every hill and mountain will be made low, the rough places will be made plain, and the crooked places will be made straight, and the glory of the Lord shall be revealed, and all flesh shall see it together.

Ben Shahn has done a drawing of Martin Luther King, in which the man seems to be part of the background of the Georgia soil and the Georgia sky. He was indeed, and this one must remember if one is to understand him, a gift of the South.

One of the sad things about America today is that the South, which has so much to teach the North about the races living in close proximity, is unable to do so, partly as a result of its own defects, partly as a result of its own arrested development, partly because the problems in the North are not the same as the problems in the South, and partly because the terrible gap between the North and the South has not been bridged more than a century after the Civil War. That the South should at last have spoken to the North through one of its Negroes may seem a paradox or an irony. But it is merely another example of the truth in the man. With this truth within him, he took the violent rhetoric of the South – and his own was violent – and made it carry the message of non-violence.

It is strange – and important – to remember how small was the issue with which he began his struggle for the civil rights of Negroes. One night, in Montgomery, Alabama, Rosa Parks, a Negro seamstress, got on a bus and sat down near the front. Following custom, the driver ordered her to give her seat to a white man and to move to the back. She refused. 'I don't know why,' she said later. 'I was just tired. My feet hurt.' She was prosecuted and fined. Martin Luther King called his first non-violent protest: the Negro boycott of the buses. The bus company was driven to the verge of bankruptcy, and then capitulated. It desegregated its buses. Only a year before, in 1954, the US Supreme Court had ordered the desegregation of public education.

But there is something else which helps, perhaps even more forcefully to fix the time of Martin Luther King, and the context in which he acted. James Baldwin published *Notes of a Native Son* in 1957. *Nobody Knows My Name* and *Another Country* followed in 1961 and 1962. Father Malcolm Boyd has recently said of them:

At his best, what did James Baldwin achieve? He let someone white get inside his black skin (not just any black skin, but Baldwin's own). The white person had a new experience, a rather shattering, personal one. In those curious pre-movement, pre-revolution days, he found out from Baldwin how, quite precisely, it makes an absolute major difference in this society what kind of skin one wears. Then the reader, racist or liberal, bigot or paternalist, had to take a further step, face a simpler and greater truth—that skin is essentially skin.

This, of course, is precisely what the Black Power leader today denies. Skin, he says, is not essentially skin: it is mind and heart and soul and being. He proclaims his skin. He has no desire to let the white man inside his skin any more than he wishes to get inside the white man's skin. Neither Stokely Carmichael nor H. Rap Brown could use the term, 'skin deep'. They deny the common humanity which lies beneath the skin, and so logically preach *apartheid*.

Did Martin Luther King and James Baldwin, then, merely serve their hour, and have they now been overtaken? Was Martin Luther King a man for one season only, or for all seasons? No one who knew him denies that the new leaders' assertion of their 'blackness' or '*négritude*' was a deeply personal challenge to him: that he examined himself and his position with an exacting and painful rigour, before emerging, in the last few months of his life, with his old beliefs intact, still persuaded that integration, and not *apartheid*, was the right course. His march on Washington was to be a march of the poor. His opposition to the war in Viet Nam was the opposition of a pacifist. His witness was still to be the witness of a man, black or white. It could not be otherwise, unless he were to enslave himself, were to cease to act as a liberated man.

No white man can easily dismiss the furious emotions which nourish the Black Power movement, and which it in turn nourishes. Yet the white man must try to speak and act as a liberated man, too: liberated from the feelings of guilt which prevent him from offering his own views frankly. I have taken considerable trouble to read the literature of the Black Power movement, and I have not the slightest doubt that it is a reactionary one. It can lead nowhere but back. Its end can only be slavery to slavery. Separate Negro states would be slave states, in mind and temper, perhaps even in regulation. This new self-enslavement is noticeable in the most recent writings of Negroes like LeRoi Jones. Father Malcolm Boyd, again, has pointed to the new stereotype of the Negro which is being created in these post-movement, post-revolution days: 'A stereotype needs to be removed, so that underneath it a person who is an artist may find himself. . . .'

It was the black stereotype – whether created, first, by the white man or, now, by the Negro himself – which Martin Luther King consistently rejected throughout his career. He would have none of it; and he could have none of it because, to him, a stereotype was simply another form of slavery. He would no more enslave himself to a stereotype than to a slave-owner; and he would not ask his people to do so. In this, he knew them well. There is no such personality, individual or collective, as *the* American Negro. Martin Luther King had good reason to know this: when Mayor Wagner called him to Harlem during the riots of 1964, the people there gave him a hostile reception. It was inevitable that they should do so. The cultural diversity of the American Negroes is remarkable, and there is little the Negroes of Harlem have in common with the Negroes of the SCLC (Southern Christian Leadership Conference). This is one reason why the Black Power leaders have no real base, why they move from city to city taking advantage of whatever situations they find favourable, why they are themselves so divided amongst themselves. There is no Black People to whom to give Black Power. Of all people, the American Negroes, with their diverse experiences, cannot be enslaved in a stereotype.

Martin Luther King had a base. In recent years, he stubbed his toes many times not only against the white communities of the North, but also against their black communities. His march of the poor on Washington was, essentially, a return to his true base. The marchers were to be drawn from all over the country, but their core was to come from the South, the temper was to be the temper of the South. The mule wagon which drew his body at his funeral was intentionally symbolic; and how far it seemed from the conditions – and the looting and the arson – of the Northern cities.

It does Martin Luther King no honour not to recognize the character of his base. Donald B. Gibson has recently pointed out 'the absurdity of the notion that there are Negro leaders who may speak for the Negro in the same sense that leaders of countries, communities, or religious sects, may speak for their citizens or congregations. . . .' Martin Luther King was, to this extent, a politician with a base in exactly the same way as Adam Clayton Powell is a politician with a base. The Negro in the North, in fact, has always had every reason to disclaim Martin Luther King's leadership. Yet from this narrow base – as narrow as any held by any Negro leader – he had, by the time he died, established an exceptional position, and it is this that is remarkable.

During the days after his death, I asked an American friend how he would summarize the real importance of Martin Luther King. He thought for a moment, and then said: 'I guess he was the first Negro leader to show that he had the capacity to survive. After all, there he was, fourteen years after it all began, still at the head. . . .' From the bus boycott in Montgomery to a movement which deserves to be called a revolution: and still there, was Martin Luther King. The gathering momentum of the revolution had not swept him away. He had suffered setbacks; but he never sank beneath the flood. As the revolution became more and more violent, there was every temptation for him to become more and more extreme; instead, he came back, and back again, and then back again, his views, his character, his ambitions, his position, *all unchanged*. He did not modify, nor qualify. Yet he survived. There is only one possible explanation, and of how few men in history can it be said: there was a truth in the man which no temptation could bend and no opposition could break.

What Robert Bolt says of Thomas More, in his introduction to *A Man For All Seasons*, can with the smallest adjustments be said of Martin Luther King:

. . . Thomas More, as I wrote about him, became for me a man with an adamantine sense of his own self. He knew where he began and left off, what area of himself he could yield to the encroachments of his enemies, and what to the encroachments of those he loved. It was a substantial area in both cases. . . . Since he was a clever man and a great lawyer, he was able to retire from those areas in wonderfully good order, but at length he was asked to retreat from that final area where he located his self. And there this . . . person set like metal, was overtaken by an absolutely primitive rigour, and could be no more budged than a cliff.

His followers in Atlanta held up the banner: *'Free At Last'*. One can hardly quarrel with so deeply Christian a legend for so deeply Christian a man. Yet he seemed to me the free man here on earth. He did not have to wait for the assassin to be liberated. By some marvel, born in the hills of the South, he had freed himself; and freed the rest of us a little; freed us especially from our fears.

We are all a little less slaves as a result of Martin Luther King's life.

DISCUSSION POINTS

1 Do you agree with Henry Fairlie's suggestion that Black Power is simply a new form of slavery for the black man?

2 'It's not enough to dream about freedom, you have to take action to achieve it.' Would this be a fair criticism of Martin Luther King?

3 'A man's character is more important than the colour of his skin.' Discuss.

4 What do you think of the view of racists – both black and white – that people with different coloured skins cannot live together in harmony and should therefore be segregated?

5 What is your opinion of mixed marriages?

6 'You need to be able to get inside a man's skin to be able to understand him fully.' What does this mean and do you agree?

PROJECT

Compile a list of racial and national stereotypes (the over-simple and misleading picture which one racial or national group has of another), illustrating these from novels, popular literature and newspapers along the lines adopted by George Orwell in his essay 'Boys' Weeklies' to be found in his *Collected Essays* (London Mercury Books, 1961). Then try to find out something about what psychologists and sociologists have had to say about prejudice and discrimination.

Henry Fairlie

READING

Prejudice, Gordon Allport (Doubleday Anchor, 1958). The classic book on the subject by an eminent American psychologist.

White and Coloured, Michael Banton (Jonathan Cape, 1958). A study of colour in Britain by a leading sociologist.

Commonsense About Race, Philip Mason (Gollancz, 1961). A leading spokesman on race relations puts the liberal case.

The Colour Problem, A. H. Richmond (Penguin, 1955). A sociologist looks at race relations in Britain.

Colour and Citizenship, E. J. B. Rose and others (OUP, for the Institute of Race Relations, 1969). The most comprehensive and reliable survey of race relations in Britain so far published.

Raymond Williams
Systems of mass communication

from *Communications in the Sixties*, Penguin 1962

The enormous growth of the mass media in postwar Britain and America is seen by many observers as a potential threat to individual liberty – especially limiting people's freedom of choice. Raymond Williams, in the following passage from his book *Communications in the Sixties*, is particularly concerned with the way in which excessive commercialism in the mass media can act as a threat to democratic freedom.

THE SYSTEMS

Perhaps it comes down to this: either the communication system is controlled or it is free. In a democracy there can be no argument on this point: the system must be free or there is no democracy. In a free system many of the things produced may be bad or offensive, or may seem bad and offensive to some people. But the only alternative is a controlled system, or monopoly, in which some people are imposing their tastes on others. 'In fact,' said Sir Robert Fraser, Head of the Independent Television Authority, defending the introduction of commercial television, 'the old system of monopoly in Britain was carried away by a wave of democratic thought and feeling.'

It would be easy to score debating points against Sir Robert Fraser: to ask, for example, what 'a wave of democratic thought and feeling' has in common with the actual process of pressure-group lobbying, much of it by persons with a direct financial interest, which got commercial television through. But this is not the main issue, since behind all the detail of contemporary controversy lies an evident conflict of principles, which has to be faced and understood.

In one way, the basic choice is between control and freedom, but in actual terms it is more often a choice between a measure of control and a measure of freedom, and the substantial argument is about how these can be combined. Further, the bare words 'controlled' and 'free' do not seem sufficiently precise, in themselves, to describe the kinds of communication system which we have had or known about or wanted. I believe that we can distinguish four main kinds, and that to describe and compare these will make our thinking about control and freedom more realistic. The four kinds are: authoritarian, paternal, commercial, and democratic.

Authoritarian

In this system, communications are seen as part of the total machine through which a minority governs a society. The first purpose of communication is to transmit the instructions, ideas, and attitudes of the ruling group. As a matter of policy, alternative instructions, ideas, and attitudes are excluded. Monopoly of the means of communication is a necessary part of the whole political system: only certain printers, publishing houses, newspapers, theatres, broadcasting stations will be allowed. Sometimes these will be directly controlled by the ruling group, who will then directly decide what is transmitted. At other times, a more indirect control will be completed by a system of censorship, and often by a system of political and administrative action against sources unfavourable to those in power.

Such a system can operate with varying degrees of severity, and in the interest of several different kinds of society. We can see it in past periods in Britain as clearly as in modern totalitarian states. The distinguishing characteristic of such a system is that the purpose of communication is to protect, maintain, or advance a social order based on minority power.

Paternal

A paternal system is an authoritarian system with a conscience: that is to say, with values and purposes beyond the maintenance of its own power. Authoritarians, on various grounds, claim the right to rule. In a paternal system, what is asserted is the duty to protect and guide. This involves the exercise of control, but it is a control directed towards the development of the majority in ways thought desirable by the minority. If monopoly of the means of communication is used, it is argued that this is to prevent the means being abused by groups which are destructive or evil. Censorship is widely used, in such a system, both directly and indirectly, but it is defended on the grounds that certain groups and individuals need, in their own interest and in the public interest, protection against certain kinds of art or ideas which would be harmful to them. Where the authoritarian system transmits orders, and the ideas and attitudes which will promote their acceptance, the paternal system transmits values, habits, and tastes, which are its own justification as a ruling minority, and which it wishes to extend to the people as a whole. Criticism of such values, habits, and tastes will be seen as at best a kind of rawness and inexperience, at worst a moral insurrection against a tried and trusted way of life. The controllers of a paternal system see themselves as guardians. Though patient, they must be uncompromising in defence of their central values. At the same time, the proper discharge of their duty requires a high sense of responsibility and seriousness. At different times, and serving different social orders, the paternal system can vary in the degree to which it explicitly announces its role or explains its methods. The actual methods can also vary widely: sometimes putting the blanket over everything; sometimes allowing a measure of controlled dissent or tolerance as a safety-valve. But the general purpose and atmosphere of the system remain unmistakable.

Commercial

The commercial attitude to communications is powerfully opposed to both authoritarianism and paternalism. Instead of communication being for government or for guidance, it is argued that men have the right to offer for sale any kind of work, and that all men have the right to buy any kind that is offered. In this way, it is claimed, the freedom of communication is assured. You do not have to ask anybody's leave to publish or to read. Works are openly offered for sale and openly bought, as people actually choose.

In its early stages, and in some of its later stages, such a system is certainly a means to freedom by comparison with either of the former systems. But since this freedom depends on the market it can run into difficulties. Can a work be offered for sale if there is no certainty that people will in fact buy it? When production is cheap, this risk will often be taken. When production is expensive, it may not be. In a modern system of communications many kinds of production are inevitably expensive. What, then, happens to the simple original principle? First: works whose sale is uncertain, or likely to be very small in relation to cost, may not be offered at all. Second: speed of sale becomes an important factor – it is not easy to wait for years for a return on a very large investment if the act of buying and selling is the most important consideration. Investment elsewhere might bring much quicker returns. Third: if the amount of capital needed to finance a work is large, there can be no free offering for sale, as in the original principle. Individual artists will almost certainly not possess the necessary capital. They have then to be financed by individuals or groups with such capital, and it is probable that considerations of extent or speed of sale, and so of return or profit on the investment, will be decisive as to whether such an offer of financing is made. But then practical control of the means of communications, over large areas and particularly in the more expensive kinds, can pass to individuals or groups whose main, if not only, qualification will be that they possess or can raise the necessary capital. Such groups, by the fact of this qualification, will often be quite unrepresentative of the society as a whole; they will be, in fact, a minority within it. Thus the control claimed as a matter of power by authoritarians, and as a matter of principle by paternalists, is often achieved as a matter of practice in the operation of the commercial system. Anything can be said, provided that you can afford to say it and that you can say it profitably.

Democratic

We have experienced the other three systems, but the democratic system, in any full sense, we can only discuss and imagine. It shares with the early commercial system a definition of communication which insists that all men have the right to offer what they choose and to receive what they choose. It is firmly against authoritarian control of what can be said, and against paternal control of what ought to be said. But also it is against commercial control of what can profitably be said, because this also can be a tyranny.

All proposals for new systems appear abstract, and at times unconvincing, because it is only when they are put into practice that they can be felt to be real. The working out of any democratic system will obviously be long and difficult, but what matters first is to define the general nature of a cultural system compatible with democracy, since there is only any chance of success in building it if enough of us can agree that this is the kind of thing we want.

There are two related considerations: the right to transmit and the right to receive. It must be the basis of any democratic culture, first, that these are basic rights; second, that they can never be tampered with by minorities; third, that if they are ever in any way limited, by some majority decision of the society, this can happen only after open and adequate public discussion, to which all are free to contribute and which will remain open to challenge and review.

On the right to transmit, the basic principle of democracy is that since all are full members of the society, all have the right to speak as they wish or find. This is not only an individual right, but a social need, since democracy depends on the active participation and the free contribution of all its members. The right to receive is complementary to this: it is the means of participation and of common discussion.

The institutions necessary to guarantee these freedoms must clearly be of a public-service kind, but it is very important that the idea of public service should not be used as a cover for a paternal or even authoritarian system. The idea of public service must be detached from the idea of public monopoly, yet remain public service in the true sense. The only way of achieving this is to create new kinds of institution.

The principle should be that the active contributors have control of their own means of expression. In the case of contributors not immediately dependent on institutions, this means guaranteeing them, if they want, certain facilities which will be their means of living and working. In cases where the work can only be done through institutions, it means creating the opportunity for the setting up, by various working groups, of their own companies, which will then be guaranteed the facilities they need. Some of these guarantees can be given by various intermediate institutions, themselves not dependent or directly dependent on the organs of government. But probably the greater part of the necessary resources will have to come directly from public funds. It is then necessary to create intermediate bodies, including representatives of the public and of the companies, to hold these public resources in trust for the society as a whole and for the needs of the various companies.

There should be no direct control by government over contributors.

The creation of intermediate bodies, and of a contractual system by which individuals and companies are guaranteed certain resources for the work they want to do, can in practice make governmental control impossible, so long as the general life of the society remains democratic. In any system, if general democracy goes, cultural democracy will go too. But while there is general democracy (in defence of which an active cultural democracy is continually necessary) what matters most is a clear acceptance of the principle that the resources exist for the contributors to use for the work they themselves want to do, and that all decisions about the actual allocation of resources should be publicly argued and open to challenge and review.

There are two difficulties in this principle, certain also to be difficult in practice. The case for control by the contributors is that the society cannot by any means be better served than by giving the contributors their freedom and the necessary resources to work with. Control by functionless financial groups, or by political or administrative factions, is certain to be damaging. But will there, can there be no control at all: either by the allocation of resources to this work rather than that, or by any measures thought generally necessary to protect the public interest?

A democratic culture would need to allot considerable resources, to keep the first danger small. It would need in any case to resist any tendency to restrict work to its own channels, however adequate. If, even in the most enlightened system, an individual or a group cannot get support, it must be quite clear that there is nothing to stop them working in any way they can, and offering their work in any way they can: a situation in which they would be much as now. The more difficult aspect of this question is that a healthy culture depends on growth, yet at any given moment new kinds of work may command little interest, and there might be considerable public pressure to give them little or no support. How can this be overcome, in any democratic way? There is no simple answer, and the only possible answer is that if it is of the nature of democratic culture that it keeps the channels of growth clear, it is a public duty to see that individuals or groups offering new kinds of work are given at least a fair chance. The problem is really one of holding the ring, to give new work the time (it will often be a long time) to prove itself. The more varied the organization, the more independent companies there are, the more this chance is likely to be given.

The second difficulty is severe. We have seen how in certain cases it can be deeply held that there are certain things which ought not to be offered, because they are likely, on the available evidence, to harm people. Will not such restrictions have to be made? Even if they are publicly argued, publicly decided, and continually open to review, are they not still restrictions? Is not paternalism in some form necessary after all? In fact, of course, if it is a majority decision it is not paternalism. But it will still feel like it, to those affected. Again, there is no simple answer to this. The general issues, and all particular cases, need continual discussion. I believe that with the pressure of profit lifted there would be less work of this difficult kind. Yet there would always be some, and you might get a majority decision against serious work. The only way to prevent this is to promote the most open discussion, including the contributor's own reasoning, or reasoning on his behalf. I do not believe that, when this is done, people usually choose wrongly. In any event, one case lost is often the next case won, for in arguing the cases there is a real growth of understanding.

It seems to be best to let the contribution be made, and let the contributor take responsibility for it. The curious situation now, in a commercial culture, is that the contributor is often neither free nor responsible: neither doing what he would independently have done, nor answerable to public criticism for what he has actually done. The balance inherent in democracy requires the creation of both these new conditions: freedom to do and freedom to answer, as an active process between many individuals.

SUMMARY

The four systems described, authoritarian, paternal, commercial, and democratic, are all to some extent active, in practice or in local experiment, in contemporary Britain. The vestiges of authoritarianism are there, in certain kinds of censorship; the first experiments in democracy are also there, in local ways. But the main struggle, over the last generations, has been between the paternal and commercial systems, and it looks as if the commercial has been steadily winning. It is most important, in this situation, that we should not confine the debate to the limited contrast of 'controlled' and 'free' systems, but instead should look over the whole range, and into detailed comparisons and possibilities.

DISCUSSION POINTS

1 Which of the four systems outlined by Raymond Williams do you think guarantees the maximum amount of free expression and free dissemination of information?

2 Discuss the view that censorship is necessary to protect society from undesirable influences.

3 'Men have the right to offer for sale any kind of work and all men have the right to buy any kind that is offered.' Do you agree?

4 Williams seems to argue that a commercial system of mass communications is a threat to freedom of expression, since only that which is profitable is permitted, and the result is a mass of cheap popular entertainment and death to the true artist. What do *you* think?

5 Consider the view that the ends of democracy are best served by public service communications institutions.

6 What do you think of the view that agencies of mass communication should be independent of both governmental *and* commercial interests?

PROJECT

Compare an issue of the *Radio Times* with the same week's issue of *T.V. Times*. Analyse each one in terms of the amount of time given to different kinds of programme; how much to plays, current affairs programmes, discussions, popular entertainment and quiz-type programmes. If possible, obtain an American newspaper and look at the kinds of programmes advertised to the public by different television networks. Compare the content of television in the U.S. with that in Britain.

READING

Television and the Child, Hilde Himmelweit, A. N. Oppenheim and Pamela Vance (OUP, 1958).
A book which tries to answer the question of what effects T.V. may have on the susceptible mind of the child.

Understanding Media, Marshall McLuhan (Routledge, 1964). What effects have the expanding mass media had on mankind? McLuhan's answer is strange and to some disturbing.

The Medium is the Massage, Marshall McLuhan (Penguin, 1967). A short exposition of McLuhan's ideas in words and pictures.

Film

The film *Face In the Crowd* is the story of a country entertainer who turns cynical manipulator on commercial radio and television.

Kenneth Tynan
The censor's gag

from *Tynan Right and Left*, Longmans Green & Co., 1967

From the early part of the eighteenth century until 1968 plays presented to the public in England and Wales had to be passed by a Lord Chamberlain. He had the power to ban plays altogether or to demand that parts of them be altered or cut out completely. Despite his picturesque title, he was nothing more nor less than a censor. Those who supported his continued existence thought that the public should be protected from certain ideas and spectacles for 'their own good'. Those opposing him argued, among other things, that there is no room for censorship in a democratic society where people should be free to choose for themselves what they saw in the theatre and to decide for themselves whether or not they agreed with a playwright's moral point of view. Many of the Chamberlain's bans, it was argued, seemed to be aimed at political rather than moral ideas in plays, and, in any case, most Chamberlains had no experience of the theatre and all too often destroyed a work of art when they set to work on it with their blue pencils.

At the forefront of the movement to remove theatre censorship was Kenneth Tynan, drama-critic and literary manager of the National Theatre, from whose book *Tynan Right and Left* the following passage is taken.

The arch-fiends were Ibsen and Shaw – social critics who brutally exposed the hypocrisies of official morality and their destructive effect on personal relationships. Both suffered from the censor's gag. 'I have studied Ibsen's plays pretty carefully,' said the Chamberlain's Examiner in 1891, 'and all the characters appear to me morally deranged.' Two years later he ambushed Shaw by banning *Mrs Warren's Profession*; and when he died in 1895, Shaw wrote a cruel and classic obituary:

The late Mr Piggot is declared on all hands to have been the best reader of plays we have ever had; and yet he was a walking compendium of vulgar insular prejudice. . . . He had French immorality on the brain; he had American indecency on the brain; he had the womanly woman on the brain; he had the divorce court on the brain; he had 'not before a mixed audience' on the brain; his official career in relation to the higher drama was one long folly and panic. . . . It is a frightening thing to see the great thinkers, poets and authors of modern Europe – men like Ibsen, Wagner, Tolstoy and the leaders of our own literature – delivered into the vulgar hands of such a noodle as this amiable old gentleman – this despised, incapable old official – most notoriously was.

Seventy years have passed since then, but appallingly little has changed. Less than a decade ago, the Chamberlain stamped on Arthur Miller's *A View from the Bridge* and Tennessee Williams's *Cat on a Hot Tin Roof* because he thought them tainted with homosexuality. These ludicrous bans have now been lifted, but the censor still forbids all theatrical representations of queer characters who follow their sexual leanings without being tragically punished or revealing any sense of guilt. Everything remotely anal, no matter how far removed from sensual enjoyment, is automatically prohibited. In 1964 the Royal Shakespeare Company (Patron: the Queen) put on a French surrealist play of the 1920s in which a stately Edwardian beauty, symbolizing death, was required to break wind at regular intervals. The stage directions indicated that the effect could be made by a bass trombone in the wings, but this was not precise enough for the Chamberlain. He passed the script only when the director agreed to let the trombonist play the Destiny Theme from Beethoven's *Fifth Symphony*. This apparently made farting respectable.

John Osborne, probably the most important British dramatist since Shaw, has naturally been singled out for the censor's special attention. His first play, an assault on McCarthyism, was presented by a provincial repertory company in 1951; it contained a scene in which one of the characters was falsely smeared as a homosexual. The Chamberlain cut the imputation of queerness and thus crippled the play. 'It's the sheer humiliation that's bad for the artist,' Osborne said to me not long ago. 'I know playwrights who almost seem to be living with the Lord Chamberlain – it's like an affair. There's a virgin period when you aren't aware of him, but eventually you can't avoid thinking of him while you're writing. He sits on your shoulder, like a terrible nanny.'

In 1959 Osborne wrote and directed a musical called *The World of Paul Slickey*. Before it opened on tour, the usual exchange of letters with the censor had taken place, including the following concession from Osborne's lawyer:

My client is prepared to substitute for:

> 'Leaping from the bridal bed,
> He preferred his youthful squire instead,'

the line

> 'He preferred the *companionship* of his
> youthful squire instead.'

But while the show was on its way to London the Chamberlain received one or two complaints that prompted him to demand new cuts and revisions. Among several offending lines, there was a lyric that ran

> And before I make a pass,
> I'll tell her that the sun shines out of her – face.

On this the censor's comment was curt and final. 'If the pause before 'face' is retained, this couplet will be unacceptable.' Osborne came down in fury to register a general protest:

Your office seems intent on treating me as if I were the producer of a third-rate nude revue. What I find most bewildering is the lack of moral consistency and objectivity which seems to characterise your recent decisions – decisions which seem to be reversed and changed because of the whim of any twisted neurotic who cares to write to you and exploit his own particular sexual frustration or moral oddity. In paying attention to what is without question an infinitesimal and lunatic minority, you are doing a grave injustice not only to myself but to the general public and your own office.

I sympathize with Osborne's rage, while regretting that he let it trap him into implying that special privileges should be granted to serious drama and withheld from 'third-rate nude revues'. Erotic stimulation is a perfectly legitimate function of bad art as well as good, and a censor who bans a stripper is behaving just as illiberally and indefensibly as one who eviscerates a masterpiece.

Osborne returned to the attack in 1960, when the Chamberlain blue-pencilled eighteen passages – many of them entire speeches – from the chronicle play, *Luther*, in which Albert Finney was to conquer the West End and Broadway. Osborne stated his terms in a white-hot letter to the London producer:

I cannot agree to any of the cuts demanded, *under any circumstances*. Nor will I agree to any possible substitutions. I don't write plays to have them re-written by someone else. I intend to make a clear unequivocal stand on this because (*a*) I think it is high time that someone did so, and (*b*) . . . the suggested cuts or alternatives would result in such damage to the psychological structure, meaning and depth of the play that the result would be a travesty. . . . I will not even contemplate any compromise . . . I am quite prepared to withdraw the play from production altogether and wait for the day when Lord Scarbrough [at that time the Lord Chamberlain] is no more. . . . I have made up my mind and, in fact, did so long ago.

This blast had its effect. For once, the censor crumpled; and *Luther* went on with only five small verbal changes, three of them involving the substitution of 'urine' or 'kidney juice' for 'piss'. Osborne wrote to the producer congratulating him on an 'astonishing victory'. His present belief, shared by most of his contemporaries in the British theatre, is that censorship is not only offensive but superfluous: The existing laws relating to libel and obscenity are already ferocious enough to warm any bigot's heart, and constitute, in themselves, quite a sizeable deterrent to freedom of speech. Would Osborne allow a Black Muslim Play to be performed in a community of white supremacists? 'Yes – anything that creates energy and vitality is good for the theatre.' When I posed the ultimate question – would he permit sexual intercourse on stage? – Osborne replied: 'It might make me ill, and I'd like to know beforehand what I was in for. But I'm prepared to be exposed to it – although I might want a seat on the aisle.'

Improvisation – the utterance of words unfiltered by the authorized sin-sieve – is one of the Chamberlain's abiding hates. A few years ago, when the off-Broadway revue called *The Premise* came to London, he forbade the cast to improvise, despite the fact that at least half of the show (according to its publicity) was made up on the moment's spur. On this occasion, mindful perhaps of Anglo-American relations, he took no legal action; but in 1958 there were convictions and fines when the producers of a play entitled *You Won't Always Be on Top* enhanced the text with an unlicensed impersonation of Sir Winston Churchill opening a public lavatory.

With these anomalies in mind, consider an antic sequence of events which unfolded in April 1965. The management of an Australian revue called *Guarding the Change* was instructed by the Chamberlain, three hours before the curtain was due to rise at the New Lyric Theatre in London, that two sketches would have to be omitted. One concerned Scott of the Antarctic, who died half a century ago, and the other was a parody of a characteristically radiant royal address which ended with the words:

Our thoughts/good wishes/carpet salesmen/aircraft carriers are on their way toward you. And so, on this beautiful morning/afternoon/evening, what is there for us to say but hello/how-do-you-do/goodbye/well done/arise, Sir Robert Menzies.

This, like the bit about Scott, was expunged on the grounds of good taste. The management at once telephoned to ask whether they could fill the gap left in their programme by reading to the audience the letter in which the Chamberlain imposed his ban. The request was refused. 'Without fear or favour,' as a wag later remarked, 'the Lord Chamberlain also banned his own letter.'

That same evening, however, the royal family themselves were rocking with laughter at an inspired Irish clown named Spike Milligan, most of whose gags are famously impromptu. To quote at length the wag cited above (Michael Frayn of *The Observer*):

They were at the Comedy Theatre, watching *Son of Oblomov*, with Spike Milligan departing from the script to make jokes in which he mentioned their names, like 'Why does Prince Philip wear red, white and blue braces?' (Answer: 'To keep his trousers up.') . . . But the point is, what is the Lord Chamberlain going to do about Mr Milligan? Mentioning Prince Philip or his braces on the West End stage is not allowed. . . . And what will he do about the royal family? If the reporters saw correctly through their night glasses in the darkness, the whole party seem to have aided and abetted Mr Milligan by providing sensible evidence of appreciation. In other words, they are all accessories after the fact Will the Lord Chamberlain revoke *their* licences? . . .

Mr Milligan has in his files what may well be the strangest single document in the history of theatre censorship. In 1962 he collaborated with John Antrobus on a clearly deranged but maniacally funny comedy called *The Bed-Sitting Room*. In January 1963, the joint authors received a communication from the Lord Chamberlain, from which I quote:

This Licence is issued on the understanding that the following alterations are made to the script:

Act I

Page 1   Omit the name of the Prime Minister: no representation of his voice is allowed.

Page 16   Omit '. . . clockwork Virgin Mary made in Hong Kong, whistles the Twist.' Omit references to the Royal Family, the Queen's Christmas Message, and the Duke's shooting. . . .

Page 21   The detergent song. Omit 'You get all the dirt off the tail of your shirt.' Substitute 'You get all the dirt off the front of your shirt.'

Page 8   The mock priest must not wear a crucifix on his snorkel. It must be immediately made clear that the book the priest handles is not the Bible.

Page 10   Omit from 'We've just consummated our marriage' to and inclusive of 'a steaming hot summer's night.'

Page 13   Omit from 'In return they are willing . . .' to and inclusive of 'the Duke of Edinburgh is a wow with Greek dishes.' Substitute 'Hark ye! Hark ye! The Day of Judgment is at hand.'

Act III

Pages 12–13   Omit the song 'Plastic Mac Man' and substitute 'Oh you dirty young devil, how dare you presume to wet the bed when the po's in the room. I'll wallop your bum with a dirty great broom when I get up in the morning.'

Page 14   Omit 'the perversions of the rubber'. Substitute 'the kreurpels and blinges of the rubber'. Omit the chamber pot under bed.

No argument I have yet heard in favour of dramatic censorship is strong enough to withstand the armour-plated case against it, which I can sum up in three quotations:

To purchase freedom of thought with human blood and then delegate its exercise to a censor at £400 a year is a proceeding which must make the gods laugh. (Frank Fowell and Frank Palmer, authors of *Censorship in England*, 1912).

What, then, is to be done with the Censorship? Nothing can be simpler. Abolish it, root and branch, throwing the whole legal responsibility for plays on the author and manager, precisely as the legal responsibility for a book is thrown on the author, the printer and the publisher. The managers will not like this; their present slavery is safer and easier; but it will be good for them, and good for the Drama. (Bernard Shaw, 1909.)

Kenneth Tynan

The Stage, my Lords and the Press are two of our Out-sentries; if we remove them – if we hoodwink them – if we throw them in Fetters – the Enemy may surprise us. Therefore I must look upon the Bill now before us as a Step, and a most necessary Step too, for introducing arbitrary Power into this Kingdom. It is a Step so necessary, that if ever any future ambitious King, or guilty Minister, should form to himself so wicked a Design, he will have reason to thank us for having done so much of the work to his Hand; but such Thanks I am convinced every one of your Lordships would blush to receive – and scorn to deserve. (Lord Chesterfield to the House of Lords, 1737.)

Chesterfield was right when he carried the case against the Lord Chamberlain beyond the boundaries of dramatic art into the broader domain of civil liberties and democratic rights. The fundamental objection to censorship is not that it is exercised against artists, but that it is exercised at all.

Sixty-odd years ago, Shaw was alarmed to hear a rumour that the United States was proposing to censor the theatre. 'O my friends across the sea,' he wrote with a passion I echo today, 'remember how the censorship works in England, and DON'T.'

DISCUSSION POINTS

1   'Censorship is necessary to save the innocent from corruption.' Discuss.

2   What do you think of the view that censorship should be abolished but that plays, like films, should have 'A' or 'X' certificates if thought unsuitable for young children?

3   It is sometimes pointed out that in Sweden they censor violence but allow a great amount of sex in films; in Britain we censor the sex but allow almost any kind of violence. If there *had* to be censorship which of these two things should be cut first? Give reasons for your answer.

4   Opponents of censorship often argue that it is ridiculous for any one person to think he knows what is best for everyone else. What do you think?

5   Some people, anxious to see the end of censorship in the theatre, are nonetheless not very anxious to see the Lord Chamberlain abolished. They argue that theatre managers, frightened of a police prosecution, will be even more savage censors than he was. What do you think?

6   Are there *any* circumstances in which censorship is justifiable in a free society?

PROJECTS

1   Find out as much as you can about the present position of censorship in Britain. Can one now *publish anything*, publicly *say anything*, *film* or *act anything*? If you saw or heard anything you considered indecent or dangerous in a theatre could you do anything about it?

2   Find out as much as you can about censorship in other countries, especially those countries which consider themselves free – e.g. the U.S.A., Soviet Russia, Cuba, Denmark, South Africa.

READING

The following books present a range of views and information on censorship in different fields of communication.

The Trial of Lady Chatterley, (ed.) C. H. Rolph (Penguin, 1961).

A Propos of 'Lady Chatterley's Lover' and Other Essays, D. H. Lawrence (Penguin, 1961).

Report of the Royal Commission on the Press, 1947–49 (H.M.S.O.).

Publish and Be Damned, Hugh Cudlipp (Weidenfeld, 1953)

Dangerous Estate, Francis Williams (Longmans, 1957).

Not for Publication, Peter Lloyd (Bow Publications Ltd, 1968).

Television and the Child, Hilde T. Himmelweit, A. N. Oppenheim and Pamela Vance (O.U.P., 1958).

Family Viewing, Mildred Masheder, Anthea Holme and Anthony Higgins (Council for Children's Welfare, 1961).

Tynan Right and Left, Kenneth Tynan (Longmans Green & Co., 1967).

Freedom, The Individual and the Law, H. Street (Penguin, 1967).

Vance Packard
The depth approach

from *The Hidden Persuaders*, Longmans Green & Co., 1957

Vance Packard's *The Hidden Persuaders* deals with some of the techniques employed by advertisers to persuade not only consumers but voters, too. The following passage from the book deals with one such technique – the so-called depth approach.

This book is an attempt to explore a strange and rather exotic new area of modern life. It is about the way many of us are being influenced and manipulated – far more than we realize – in the patterns of our everyday lives. Large-scale efforts are being made, often with impressive success, to channel our unthinking habits, our purchasing decisions, and our thought processes by the use of insights gleaned from psychiatry and the social sciences. Typically these efforts take place beneath our level of awareness; so that the appeals which move us are often, in a sense, 'hidden'.

Some of the manipulating being attempted is simply amusing. Some of it is disquieting, particularly when viewed as a portent of what may be ahead on a more intensive and effective scale for us all. Cooperative scientists have come along providentially to furnish some awesome tools.

The use of mass psychoanalysis to guide campaigns of persuasion has become the basis of a multimillion-dollar industry. Professional persuaders have seized upon it in their groping for more effective ways to sell us their wares – whether products, ideas, attitudes, candidates, goals, or states of mind.

This depth approach to influencing our behaviour is being used in

124

many fields and is employing a variety of ingenious techniques. It is being used most extensively to affect our daily acts of consumption. The sale to us of billions of dollars' worth of United States products is being significantly affected, if not revolutionized, by this approach, which is still only barely out of its infancy. Two-thirds of America's hundred largest advertisers have geared campaigns to this depth approach by using strategies inspired by what marketers call 'motivation analysis'.

Meanwhile, many of the nation's leading public-relations experts have been indoctrinating themselves in the lore of psychiatry and the social sciences in order to increase their skill at 'engineering' our consent to their propositions. Fund raisers are turning to the depth approach to wring more money from us. A considerable and growing number of our industrial concerns (including some of the largest) are seeking to sift and mould the behaviour of their personnel – particularly their own executives – by using psychiatric and psychological techniques. Finally, this depth approach is showing up nationally in the professional politician's intensive use of symbol manipulation and reiteration on the voter, who more and more is treated like Pavlov's conditioned dog.

The efforts of the persuaders to probe our everyday habits for hidden meanings are often interesting purely for the flashes of revelation they offer us of ourselves. We are frequently revealed, in their findings, as comical actors in a genial if twitchy Thurberian world. The findings of the depth probers provide startling explanations for many of our daily habits and perversities. It seems that our subconscious can be pretty wild and unruly.

What the probers are looking for, of course, are the *whys* of our behaviour, so that they can more effectively manipulate our habits and choices in their favour. This has led them to probe why we are afraid of banks; why we love those big fat cars; why we really buy homes; why men smoke cigars; why the kind of car we draw reveals the brand of gasoline we will buy; why housewives typically fall into a hypnoidal trance when they get into a supermarket; why men are drawn into auto showrooms by convertibles but end up buying sedans; why junior loves cereal that pops, snaps, and crackles.

We move from the genial world of James Thurber into the chilling world of George Orwell and his Big Brother, however, as we explore some of the extreme attempts at probing and manipulating now going on.

Certain of the probers, for example, are systematically feeling out our hidden weaknesses and frailties in the hope that they can more efficiently influence our behaviour. At one of the largest advertising agencies in America psychologists on the staff are probing sample humans in an attempt to find how to identify, and beam messages to, people of high anxiety, body consciousness, hostility, passiveness, and so on. A Chicago advertising agency has been studying the housewife's menstrual cycle and its psychological concomitants in order to find the appeals that will be more effective in selling her certain food products.

Seemingly, in the probing and manipulating nothing is immune or sacred. The same Chicago ad agency has used psychiatric probing techniques on little girls. Public-relations experts are advising churchmen how they can become more effective manipulators of their congregations. In some cases these persuaders even choose our friends for us, as at a large 'community of tomorrow' in Florida. Friends are furnished along with the linen by the management in offering the homes for sale. Everything comes in one big, glossy package.

Sombre examples of the new persuaders in action are appearing not only in merchandising but in politics and industrial relations. The national chairman of a political party indicated his merchandising approach to the election of 1956 by talking of his candidates as products to sell. In many industrial concerns now the administrative personnel are psychoanalysed, and their futures all charted, by trained outside experts. And then there is the trade school in California that boasts to employers that it socially engineers its graduates so that they are, to use the phrase of an admiring trade journal, 'custom-built men' guaranteed to have the right attitudes from the employer's standpoint.

What the persuaders are trying to do in many cases was well summed up by one of their leaders, the president of the Public Relations Society of America, when he said in an address to members: 'The stuff with which we work is the fabric of men's minds.' In many of their attempts to work over the fabric of our minds the professional persuaders are receiving direct help and guidance from respected social scientists. Several social-science professors at Columbia University, for example, took part in a seminar at the university attended by dozens of New York public-relations experts. In the seminar one professor, in a sort of chalk talk, showed these manipulators precisely the types of mental manipulation they could attempt with most likelihood of success.

All this probing and manipulation has its constructive and its amusing aspects; but also, I think it fair to say, it has seriously anti-humanistic implications. Much of it seems to represent regress rather than progress for man in his long struggle to become a rational and self-guiding being. Something new, in fact, appears to be entering the pattern of American life with the growing power of our persuaders.

In the imagery of print, film, and air wave the typical American citizen is commonly depicted as an uncommonly shrewd person. He or she is dramatized as a thoughtful voter, rugged individualist, and, above all, as a careful, hardheaded consumer of the wondrous products of American enterprise. He is, in short, the flowering of twentieth-century progress and enlightenment.

Most of us like to fit ourselves into this picture, and some of us surely are justified in doing so. The men and women who hold up these glowing images, particularly the professional persuaders, typically do so, however, with tongue in cheek. The way these persuaders – who often refer to themselves good-naturedly as 'symbol manipulators' – see us in the quiet of their inter-office memos, trade journals, and shop talk is frequently far less flattering, if more interesting. Typically they see us as bundles of day-dreams, misty hidden yearnings, guilt complexes, irrational emotional blockages. We are image lovers given to impulse and compulsive acts. We annoy them with our seemingly senseless quirks, but we please them with our growing docility in responding to their manipulation of symbols that stir us to action. They have found the supporting evidence for this view persuasive enough to encourage them to turn to depth channels on a large scale in their efforts to influence our behaviour.

The symbol manipulators and their research advisers have developed their depth views of us by sitting at the feet of psychiatrists and social scientists (particularly psychologists and sociologists) who have been hiring themselves out as 'practical' consultants or setting up their own research firms. Gone are the days when these scientists confined themselves to classifying manic depressives, fitting round pegs in round holes, or studying the artifacts and mating habits of Solomon Islanders. These new experts, with training of varying thoroughness, typically refer to themselves as 'motivation analysts' or 'motivation researchers'. The head of a Chicago research firm that conducts psycho-analytically oriented studies for merchandisers, Louis Cheskin, sums up what he is doing in these candid terms:

Motivation research is the type of research that seeks to learn what motivates people in making choices. It employs techniques designed to reach the unconscious or subconscious mind because preferences generally are determined by factors of which the individual is not conscious. . . . Actually in the buying situation the consumer generally acts emotionally and compulsively, unconsciously reacting to the images and designs which in the subconscious are associated with the product.

Mr Cheskin's clients include many of America's leading producers of consumer goods.

These motivational analysts, in working with the symbol manipulators, are adding depth to the selling of ideas and products. They are learning, for example, to offer us considerably more than the actual item involved. A Milwaukee advertising executive commented to colleagues in print on the fact that women will pay two dollars and a half for skin cream but no more than twenty-five cents for a cake of soap. Why? Soap, he explained, only promises to make them clean. The cream promises to make them beautiful. (Soaps have now started promising beauty as well as cleanness.) This executive added, 'The women are buying a promise.' Then he went on to say: 'The cosmetic manufacturers are not selling lanolin, they are selling hope. . . . We no longer buy oranges, we buy vitality. We do not buy just an auto, we buy prestige.'

The reason why I mention merchandisers more frequently than the other types of persuader in this exploration is that they have more billions of dollars immediately at stake and so have been pouring more effort into pioneering the depth approach. But the others – including publicists, fund raisers, politicians, and industrial personnel experts – are getting into the field rapidly, and others with anything to promote will presumably follow.

Since our concern here is with the breed of persuaders known in the trade as the 'depth boys', much of the book is devoted to describing their subterranean operations. For that reason I should add the obvious: a great many advertising men, publicists, fund raisers, personnel experts, and political leaders, in fact numerically a majority, still do a straightforward job and accept us as rational citizens (whether we are or not). They fill an important and constructive role in our society. Advertising, for example, not only plays a vital role in promoting our economic growth but is a colourful, diverting aspect of American life; and many of the creations of ad men are tasteful, honest works of artistry.

As for the new operators in depth, some of them try for good reason to pursue their operations quietly. I frequently came up against a wall in trying to get direct information from companies known to be deeply involved in depth probing. In two cases in which officials of such companies had been candid with me they later called and confessed they had been talking out of turn. They asked me not to identify them or their companies or products, and I have respected their requests for anonymity. Others, particularly from the research organizations, were so frank and detailed about their findings and operations that while I admired their candour I at times wondered if they had become insensitive to some of the antihumanistic implications of what they were doing. Some were so cooperative in providing me with remarkable case material and explanations that I now find it embarrassing to try to relate in cold print some of what they told me. However, I shall do so and hope they will not be too offended. In justice perhaps I should add that the trade journals of the persuaders occasionally publish soul-searching commentaries on some of the manipulative practices of colleagues.

The motivational analyst and symbol manipulator pooling their talents, and with millions of dollars at their disposal, make a fascinating and at times disturbing team. Results of their manoeuvres indicate they are still quite a way from being infallible. Many of them are quick to admit their techniques are still not precise. But startling beginnings are being made.

These depth manipulators are, in their operations, beneath the surface of conscious life, starting to acquire a power of persuasion that is becoming a matter of justifiable public scrutiny and concern.

It is hoped this book may contribute to the process of public scrutiny.

DISCUSSION POINTS

1   Ought a social scientist to sell his skills and knowledge about human beings to advertisers who he knows are using it to persuade people in the way Packard describes?

2   Is *any* method of persuading people to buy goods justified?

3   In what ways might the depth approach constitute a threat to liberty and democracy?

4   'If people are persuaded by slick advertising it's their own look-out.' Discuss.

5   Should people be protected from advertisers employing the depth

approach or not? If so, what is the best method of doing this: (a) to ban its use; (b) to make as many people as possible aware of its existence through press and television; or (c) to teach children in school about the techniques advertisers employ?

6   Packard says that much of the probing and manipulating which he describes 'seems to represent regress rather than progress for man in his long struggle to become a rational self-guiding being.' What exactly does he mean, and do you agree with him?

7   Do you think that ordinary people are more hard-headed and shrewd than Packard would have us believe?

PROJECT

Examine a range of advertisements – either on hoardings, in magazines or on television – and try to classify them according to the amount of factual information about the product which they give and the kinds of 'dreams' they appeal to.

READING

The Shocking History of Advertising, R. S. Turner (Penguin, 1965). A witty and entertaining history of advertising in England and America.

The Hidden Persuaders, Vance Packard (Penguin, 1960). A rather disturbing account of mass persuasion techniques employed by some American advertisers.

The Techniques of Persuasion, J. A. C. Brown (Penguin, 1963). A psychologist looks at methods of persuasion ranging from propaganda to brainwashing.

Jacob Bronowski

Science, the destroyer or creator

from *The Common Sense of Science*, Heinemann 1951

Science has brought many benefits to individuals in advanced industrial societies, but it has also led men to search for and discover new means of waging war, means of threatening man's freedom from tyranny. Among those most aware of its potential destructive powers are many eminent scientists. Here Dr Jacob Bronowski, the distinguished British research physicist, raises the important question of whether man's cleverness has outstripped his morality.

We all know the story of the sorcerer's apprentice; or *Frankenstein* which Mary Shelley wrote in competition with her husband and Byron; or some other story of the same kind out of the macabre invention of the nineteenth century. In these stories, someone who has special powers over nature conjures or creates a stick or a machine to do his work for him; and then finds that he cannot take back the life he has given it. The mindless monster overwhelms him; and what began as an invention to do the housework ends by destroying the master with the house.

These stories have become the epitome of our own fears. We have been inventing machines at a growing pace now for about three hundred years. This is a short span even in our recorded history, and it is not a thousandth part of our history as men. In that short moment of time we have found a remarkable insight into the workings of nature. We have used it to make ourselves far more flexible in our adaptation to the outside world than any other animal has ever been. We can survive in climates which even germs find difficult. We can grow our own food and meat. We can travel overland and we can tunnel and swim and fly, all in the one body. More important than any of these, we have come nearest to the dream which Lamarck had, that animals might inherit the skills which their parents learned. We have discovered the means to record our experience so that others may live it again.

The history of other animal species shows that the most successful in the struggle for survival have been those which were most adaptable to changes in their world. We have made ourselves by means of our tools beyond all measure more adaptable than any other species, living or extinct; and we continue to do so with gathering speed. Yet today we are afraid of our own shadow in the nine o'clock news; and we wonder whether we shall survive so over-specialized a creature as the Pekinese.

Everyone likes to blame his sense of defeat on someone else; and for some time scientists have been a favourite scapegoat. I want to look at their responsibility, and for that matter at everybody's, rather more closely. They do have a special responsibility; do not let us argue that out of existence; but it is a complicated one, and it is not the whole responsibility. For example, science obviously is not responsible for the readiness of people, who do not take their private quarrels beyond the stage of insult, to carry their public quarrels to the point of war. Many animals fight for their needs, and some for their mere greeds, to the point of death. Bucks fight for females, and birds fight for their territories. The fighting habits of man are odd because he displays them only in groups. But they were not supplied by scientists. On the contrary, science has helped to end several kinds of group murder, such as witch hunting and the taboos of the early nineteenth century against disinfecting hospitals.

Neither is science responsible for the existence of groups which believe themselves to be in competition: for the existence above all of nations. And the threat of war today is always a national threat. Some bone of contention and competition is identified with a national need: Fiume or the Polish corridor or the dignity of the Austrian Empire; and in the end nations are willing to organize and to invite the death of citizens on both sides in order to reach these collective aims. Science did not create the nations; on the contrary, it has helped to soften those strong national idiosyncrasies which it seems necessary to exploit if war is to be made with enthusiasm. And wars are not made by any traditional groups: they are made by highly organized societies, they are made by nations. Most of us have seen Yorkshiremen invade Old Trafford, and a bloody nose or two if the day was thirsty. But no Yorkshireman would have grown pale if he had been told that Lancashire had the atomic bomb.

The sense of doom in us today is not a fear of science; it is a fear of war. And the causes of war were not created by science; they do not differ in kind from the known causes of the War of Jenkins' Ear or the Wars of the Roses, which were carried on with only the most modest scientific aids. No, science has not invented war; but it has turned it into a very different thing. The people who distrust it are not wrong. The man in the pub who says 'It'll wipe out the world,' the woman in the queue who says 'It isn't natural' – they do not express themselves very well; but what they are trying to say does make sense. Science has enlarged the mechanism of war, and it has distorted it. It has done this in at least two ways.

First, science has obviously multiplied the power of the warmakers. The weapons of the moment can kill more people more secretly and more unpleasantly than those of the past. This progress, as for want of another word I must call it – this progress has been going on for some time; and for some time it has been said, of each new weapon, that it is so destructive or so horrible that it will frighten people into their wits, and force the nations to give up war for lack of cannon fodder. This hope has never been fulfilled, and I know no one who takes refuge in it today. The acts of men and women are not dictated by such simple compulsions; and they themselves do not stand in any simple relation to the decisions of the nations which they compose. Grapeshot and TNT and gas have not helped to outlaw war; and I see no sign that the hydrogen bomb or a whiff of bacteria will be more successful in making men wise by compulsion.

Secondly, science at the same time has given the nations quite new occasions for falling out. I do not mean such simple objectives as someone else's uranium mine, or a Pacific Island which happens to be knee-deep in organic fertilizer. I do not even mean merely another nation's factories and her skilled population. These are all parts of the surplus above our simple needs which they themselves help to create and which gives our civilization its character. And war in our world battens on this surplus. This is the object of the greed of nations, and this also gives them the leisure to train and the means to arm for war. At bottom, we have remained individually too greedy to distribute our surplus, and collectively too stupid to pile it up in any more useful form than the traditional mountains of arms. Science can claim to have created the surplus in our societies, and we know from the working day and the working diet how greatly it has increased it in the last two hundred years. Science has created the surplus. Now put this year's budget beside the budget of 1750, anywhere in the world, and you will see what we are doing with it.

I myself think there is a third dimension which science has added to modern war. It has created war nerves and the war of nerves. I am not thinking about the technical conditions for a war of nerves: the camera man and the radio and the massed display of strength. I am thinking of the climate in which this stage lightning flickers and is made to seem real. The last twenty years have given us a frightening show of these mental states. There is a division in the mind of each of us, that has become plain, between the man and the brute; and the rift can be opened, the man submerged, with a cynical simplicity, with the meanest tools of envy and frustration, which in my boyhood would have been thought inconceivable in a civilized society. I shall come back to this cleavage in our minds, for it is much more than an item in a list of war crimes. But it is an item. It helps to create the conditions for disaster. And I think that science has contributed to it. Science; the fact that science is there, mysterious, powerful; the fact that most people are impressed by it but ignorant and helpless – all this seems to me to have contributed to the division in our minds. And scientists cannot escape the responsibility for this. They have enjoyed acting the mysterious stranger, the powerful voice without emotion, the expert and the god. They have failed to make themselves comfortable in the talk of people in the street, no one taught them the knack, of course, but they were not keen to learn. And now they find the distance which they enjoyed has turned to distrust, and the awe has turned to fear; and people who are by no means fools really believe that we should be better off without science.

These are the indictments which scientists cannot escape. Of course, they are often badly phrased, so that scientists can side-step them with generalities about the common responsibility, and who voted the credits for atomic research anyway; which are perfectly just, but not at all relevant. That is not the heart of the matter; and the people in queues and pubs are humbly groping for the heart. They are not good at saying things and they do not give model answers to interviewers. But when we say 'We've forgotten what's right,' when they say 'We're not fit to handle such things,' what is in their minds is perfectly true. Science and society are out of joint. Science has given to no one in particular a power which no one in particular knows how to use. Why do not scientists invent something sensible? Wives say it every time they stub their toe on the waste bin, and husbands say it whenever a fuse blows. Why is it the business of no one in particular to stop fitting science for death and to begin fitting it into our lives? We will agree that warlike science is no more than a by-product of a warlike society. Science has merely provided the means, for good or for bad; and society has seized it for bad. But what are we going to do about it?

The first thing to do, it seems to me, is to treat this as a scientific question: by which I mean as a practical and sensible question, which deserves a factual approach and a reasoned answer. Now that I have apologized on behalf of scientists, and this on a scale which some of them will certainly think too ample, let us cut out what usually happens to the argument at this point, the rush of recriminations. The scientists are conscious of their mistakes; and I do not want to discuss the mistakes of non-scientists – although they have made a great many – except those which we all must begin to make good.

I have said that a scientific answer must be practical as well as sensible. This really rules out at once the panaceas which also tend to run the argument into a blind alley at this stage; the panaceas which say summarily 'Get rid of them.' Naturally, it does not seem to me to be sensible to get rid of scientists; but in any case, it plainly is not practical. And whatever we do with our own scientists, it very plainly is not practical to get rid of the scientists of rival nations; because if there existed the conditions for agreement among nations on this far-reaching scheme, then the conditions for war would already have disappeared. If there existed the conditions for international agreement, say to suspend all scientific research, or to abandon warlike research, or in any other way to forgo science as an instrument of nationalism – if such agreements could be reached, then they would already be superfluous; because the conditions for war would already have disappeared. So, however we might sigh for Samuel Butler's panacea in *Erewhon*, simply to give up all machines, there is no point in talking about it. I believe it would be a disaster for mankind like the coming of the Dark Ages. But there is no point in arguing this. It just is not practical, nationally or internationally.

There are no panaceas at all; and we had better face that. There is nothing that we can do overnight, in a week or a month, which can straighten by a laying on of hands the ancient distortion of our society. Do not let us fancy that any one of us out of the blue will concoct that stirring letter to *The Times* which will change the black mood of history – and the instructions to diplomats. Putting scientists in the Cabinet will not do that, and women in the War Office will not, nor will bishops in the Privy Council. There are no panaceas. We are the heirs to a tradition which has left science and society out of step. The man in the street is right: we have never learned to handle such things. Nothing will do but that we learn. But learning is not done in a year. Our ultimate survival is in our own hands. Our survival while we are learning is a much chancier thing. We had better be realistic about that.

Meanwhile we had better settle down to work for our ultimate survival; and we had better start now. We have seen that the diagnosis has turned out to be not very difficult. Science and our social habits are out of step. And the cure is no deeper either. We must learn to match them. And there is no way of learning this unless we learn to understand *both*.

Of the two, of course, the one which is strange is science. I have already blamed the scientist for that. He has been the monk of our age, timid, thwarted, anxious to be asked to help; and with a secret ambition to play the Grey Eminence. Through years of childhood poverty he dreamed of this. Scientific skill was a blue door beckoning to him, which would open into the society of dignitaries of state. But the private motives of scientists are not the trend of science. The trend of science is made by the needs of society: navigation before the eighteenth century, manufacture thereafter; and in our age I believe the liberation of personality. Whatever the part which scientists like to act, or for that matter which painters like to dress, science shares the aims of our society just as art does. The difficulties of understanding either are not fundamental; they are difficulties only of language. To grow familiar with the large ideas of science calls for patience and an effort of attention; and I hope I have shown that it repays them.

For two hundred years, these ideas have been applied to technical needs; and they have made our world anew, triumphantly, from top to toe. Our shoes are tanned and stitched, our clothes are spun and dyed and woven, we are lighted and carried and doctored by means which were unknown to neat Mr Pope at Twickenham in 1740. We may not think that is much to put against the eighty thousand dead in Hiroshima, or we may. We may not think it recompenses us for the absence of any Mr. Pope from Twickenham today; we may even hold it responsible. It is certainly not a spiritual achievement. But it has not yet tried to be. It has applied its ideas monotonously to shoe-leather and bicycle bells. And it has made a superb job of them. Compare its record in its own field with that of any other ideas of the same age: Burke's ideas of the imagination, or Bentham's on government, or Adam Smith on political economy. If any ideas have a claim to be called creative, because they have created something, then certainly it is the ideas of science.

We may think that all that science has created is comfort; and it certainly has done that – the very word 'comfortable' in the modern sense dates from the Industrial Revolution. But have we always stopped to think what science has done not to our mode of living but to our life? We talk about research for death, the threat of war and the number of civilians who get killed. But have we always weighed this against the increase in our own life span? Let us do a small sum. The number of people killed in Great Britain in six years of war by German bombs, flying bombs, and V2's was sixty thousand. They were an average lot of people, which means that on an average they lost half their expectation of life. Quite an easy long division shows that the effect of this in our population of fifty million people was to shorten the average span of life by less than one tenth of one per cent. This is considerably less than a fortnight. Put this on the debit side. And on the credit side, we know that in the last hundred years the average span of life in England has increased by twenty years. That is the price of science, take it or leave it – a fortnight for twenty years of life. And these twenty years have been created by applying to daily life, to clothing and bedding, to hygiene and infection, to birth and death, the simple ideas of science – the fundamental ideas I have been talking about: order, cause, and chance. If any ideas have a claim to be called creative, because they have created life, it is the ideas of science.

We have not neglected these ideas altogether in our social organization. But, it is a point I have made several times, we have got hopelessly behind with them. The idea of order is now old enough to have reached at least our filing cabinets. The idea of cause and effect has entered our habits, until it has become the new *a priori* in the making of administrative plans. The difficulty is to dislodge it, now that it is hardening into a scholastic formula. For the idea which has given a new vigour to science in our generation is larger than the machinery of cause and effect. It stipulates no special mechanism between the present and the future. It is content to predict the future, without insisting that the computation must follow the steps of causal law. I have called this the idea of chance, because its method is statistical, and because it recognizes that every prediction carries with it its own measurable uncertainty. A good prediction is one which defines its area of uncertainty; a bad prediction ignores it. And at bottom this is no more than the return to the essentially empirical, the experimental nature of science. Science is a great many things, and I have called them a great many names; but in the end they all return to this: science is the acceptance of what works and the rejection of what does not. That needs more courage than we might think.

It needs more courage than we have ever found when we have faced our worldly problems. This is how society has lost touch with science: because it has hesitated to judge itself by the same impersonal code of what works and what does not. We have clung to Adam Smith and Burke, or we have agitated for Plato or Aquinas, through wars and famine, through rising and falling birth-rates, and through libraries of learned argument. And in the end, our eyes have always wandered from the birth-rate to the argument: from the birth-rate to what we have wanted to believe. Here is the crux of what I have been saying. Here is our ultimate hope of saving ourselves from extinction. We must learn to understand that the content of all knowledge is empirical; that its test is whether it works; and we must learn to act on that understanding in the world as well as in the laboratory.

This is the message of science: our ideas must be realistic, flexible, unbigoted – they must be human, they must create their own authority. If any ideas have a claim to be creative, because they have liberated that creative impulse, it is the ideas of science.

This is not only a material code. On the contrary, my hope is that it may heal the spiritual cleft which two wars have uncovered. I have seen in my lifetime an abyss open in the human mind: a gulf between the endeavour to be man, and the relish in being brute. The scientist has indeed had a hand in this, and every other specialist too, with his prim detachment and his oracular airs. But of course, the large strain which has opened this fault is social. We have made men live in two halves, a Sunday half and a workday half. We have ordered them to love their neighbour and to turn the other cheek, in a society which has constantly compelled them to shoulder their neighbour aside and to turn their backs. So we have created a savage sense of failure which, as we know now to our cost, can be tapped with an ease which is frightening; and which can thrust up, with explosive force, a symbol to repeat to any unhappy people its most degrading dream.

Can science heal that neurotic flaw in us? If science cannot, then nothing can. Let us stop pretending. There is no cure in high moral precepts. We have preached them too long to men who are forced to live how they can: *that* makes the strain which they have not been able to bear. We need an ethic which is moral *and* which works. It is often said that science has destroyed our values and put nothing in their place. What has really happened of course is that science has shown in harsh relief the division between our values and our world. We have not begun to let science get into our heads; where then was it supposed to create these values? We have used it as a machine without will, the conjured spirit to do the chores. I believe that science can create values: and will create them precisely as literature does, by looking into the human personality; by discovering what divides it and what cements it. That is how great writers have explored man, and this whether they themselves as men have been driven by the anguish in *Gulliver's Travels* or the sympathy in *Moll Flanders*. The insight of science is not different from that of the arts. Science will create values, I believe, and discover virtues, when it looks into man; when it explores what makes him man and not an animal, and what makes his societies human and not animal packs.

I believe that we can reach this unity in our culture. I began this book by recalling that nations in their great ages have not been great in art or science, but in art and science. Rembrandt was the contemporary of Huygens and Spinoza. At that very time, Isaac Newton walked with Dryden and Christopher Wren. We know that ours is a remarkable age of science. It is for us to use it to broaden and to liberate our culture. These are the marks of science: that it is open for all to hear, and all are free to speak their minds in it. They are marks of the world at its best, and the human spirit at its most challenging.

DISCUSSION POINTS

1 Has science been an aid or a hindrance to man's moral progress?

2 'It would have been better if the scientists who first learned how to split the atom had kept quiet about it; if they had, at least we would not be living in fear of nuclear war.' Discuss.

3   Consider the view that it is ignorance, greed and nationalism that cause wars and that science, if anything, works to diminish these things and hence to lessen the possibility of war.

4   Bronowski argues that the scientific approach to the world rules out panaceas which say summarily 'Get rid of them.' Is the scientific approach compatible with political or moral extremism?

5   'The answer to most of our problems would be something quite simple, like giving up all machines.' Do you agree with such a view or do you think there is some other *simple* solution to *all* our problems?

6   What do you think of the idea that knowledge is power?

7   Some people would argue that even one life lost is too great a price to pay for scientific advance and the comfort it has brought to many of us. What do you think?

8   'Science is the acceptance of what works and the rejection of what does not.' Do you agree with this and do you think that this applies also in the sphere of morals and politics?

9   'This is the message of science: our ideas must be realistic, flexible, unbigoted – they must be human, they must create their own authority. If any ideas have a claim to be called creative, because they have liberated that creative impulse, it is the ideas of science.' (Bronowski.) How important is liberty to the scientist and the future progress of science?

10   'In order to be great a nation needs to be great in both art *and* science.' This is Bronowski's view. Look at the reasons he gives in support of this opinion and then say whether or not you agree, giving your own reasons.

PROJECT

Write a science fiction account of life in 2000 A.D. bringing out the benefits and destructive potentialities of modern science.

READING

The World in 1984, Nigel Calder (ed.), (Penguin, 1965, 2 vols). A hundred different international experts take a look into the future.

The Rise of the Meritocracy, Michael Young (Penguin, 1961). A sociologist considers the kind of society in which we are likely to find ourselves living in 2034 A.D. – a society ruled by meritocrats.

Silent Spring, Rachel Carson (Penguin, 1965). A disturbing report of the contaminating effects of pesticides on our food.

Cat's Cradle, Kurt Vonnegut (Penguin, 1965). One of the 'fathers' of the atomic bomb leaves his three children another lethal legacy – a chip of the deadly *Ice-nine*. This novel tells the story of what happens when the stuff gets loose. The author is a biochemist turned novelist.

Richard Davy
Students in Revolt

from *The Times*, June 1, 1968

Recent years have seen a sudden and widespread upsurge of student unrest. The United States, France, Germany, Mexico and Japan have been the scene of perhaps the most violent clashes between students and the authorities, and similar if less bloody disturbances in Britain have led some sections of opinion to the view that students are abusing what is seen as a privileged position. After all, it is argued, students are financed by the taxpayer so the taxpayer has every right to expect them to earn their keep by working hard and not to waste their time protesting. The students, on the other hand, argue that democracy should guarantee the fundamental right to protest and that there is much to protest against in the modern world.

Why has the so-called 'student revolution' occurred? The following passage by Richard Davy, originally written for *The Times* newspaper, tries to answer this question. It is based on material supplied by foreign correspondents of *The Times* throughout the world.

If you want to synthesize a student revolt in your laboratory proceed as follows. Take several thousand students of sociology and make them attend lectures in a hall that holds a hundred. Tell them that even if they pass their examinations there will probably be no jobs for them. Surround them with a society that does not practise what it preaches and is run by political parties that do not represent the students' ideas.

Tell them to think about what is wrong with society and how to put it right. As soon as they become actively interested in the subject send in the police to beat them up. Then stand well clear of the bang and affect an attitude of confused surprise.

This is, of course, a crude simplification but it does at least hint at the pattern of some of the student trouble in the western world – a combination of educational grievances, political disillusion, moral concern, frustration, boredom, enthusiasm and a certain amount of imitativeness.

The protesters are a small minority. Most students in most countries (except where political activity is traditional) are peaceful conformists concerned mainly with getting a degree, a spouse and a job. Even many of the activists will eventually melt quietly into a life revolving round wife and family, promotion, mortgages and other mundane cares.

This is too obvious to need any more emphasis or elaboration. But it does not dispose of the problem of student protest. There are at least two questions that need answering. First, how much real power can the protesting minority command in terms of their ability to make trouble, put pressure on authorities, and rally wider support on specific issues? Secondly, should we regard these protesters as misguided delinquents and nuisances, or as social critics with opinions that deserve serious attention? If the latter, it is irrelevant whether their views are widely held. True prophets have always been in a minority.

The first question has been largely answered by recent events. Student power has made itself felt in many different countries. No political or academic authorities in any country, even the most totalitarian, can afford wholly to ignore student feelings. Any government is now likely to think twice before sending its police on to university premises. Any university administration is likely to hesitate before disciplining students or refusing requests for student representation.

Many are trying to ward off trouble by inviting students to play more part in university affairs. Governments are waking up to the fact that they have greatly underestimated the educational crisis which modern industrial society creates for itself.

The second question – whether the protesters have anything valid to say – is again partly answered by events. The militant students have been able to get large numbers out into the streets and in some countries have won a good deal of public support. No matter how adept they are at agitation they could not do this if they represented absolutely nothing and nobody but themselves, and if they were acting in an atmosphere of total isolation and hostility. Which does not mean that they have wide support for their specific revolutionary ideas.

Richard Davy

Long tradition

There is, however, no need to become too much tied up with the details
of revolutionary arguments. After all, the radicals themselves disagree
a lot about doctrine. It is probably more useful to stand back a little
and recognize that most student radicals are not screaming delinquents
but highly intelligent, interesting and often charming people.

Their arguments may often be questionable, their experience short,
and their methods distasteful, but what they are doing, in effect, is
uttering a cry of distress and anger at some aspects of modern society.
They are in the long tradition of protest against injustice, hypocrisy,
oppression and materialism. They need not be ignored just because
they do not produce careful working papers on constitutional reform.

Their protest usually starts from very real shortcomings in the educational systems of the countries involved.

As we said at the beginning of this series, the student population of
the world is exploding. It is likely to go on doing so. In Britain alone
it has been estimated that the number of people in higher education
may double again between now and 1980. Apart from the demands that
this will make on facilities, it will increase the already unhealthy degree
to which education becomes a closed circuit affair, with more and more
graduates being brought back to become teachers.

Except where powerful political factors are involved, there seems to
be a clear correlation between student radicalism and educational crisis.
There may even be a correlation with staff-student ratios. This would
be difficult to prove, but the average British ratio is about 1:10. At the
Sorbonne it is about 1:98. At the Free University of Berlin it is about
1:50, reaching 1:300 in some popular subjects.

Numbers are not the only problem. The whole role of the university
in society and in politics is more confused than ever before. In advanced
as well as developing societies its main function is no longer to produce
a small ruling élite educated mostly in the humanities. Nor can it give
first priority to the disinterested pursuit of knowledge.

It has become a vital industry that must produce a certain quantity
of people trained to certain specifications if the nation is to prosper. It
must take in a vast new class of students whose family backgrounds are
often remote from the traditions of university life and higher learning.
The student has become raw material in the processing plant. Even
then he does not always get full attention. The university is also called
upon to turn out knowledge for government, industry, or the defence

144

establishment. Since this can bring in quicker returns than teaching undergraduates it sometimes gets priority.

These basic problems are common to a great many countries. In the United States the student feels them mostly in the size and impersonality of the universities and in the neglect of undergraduate teaching. Berkeley has 27,431 undergraduates, and a frequent complaint is that 'I'm only a number'. The pressures of commerce and the Pentagon are also felt as corrupting by many students.

In Europe size is also a problem. There are 125,000 students at the Sorbonne, 15,100 at the Free University of Berlin, and 63,000 in Rome. To make matters worse, the structure of some universities remains largely in the nineteenth century, with professors forming a small, self-perpetuating and autocratic ruling class, often with a vested interest in the status quo – a classic revolutionary situation. West Germany provides one example.

France has similar problems with its mandarin system, producing scholarly arts graduates who then cannot get jobs. There is intense overcrowding, shortage of facilities, and books, severe, often irrelevant academic demands, and practically no contact at all with the professors.

British students are comparatively well off, which partly accounts for the quieter atmosphere, but even here universities are growing bigger, teachers are beginning to neglect their pastoral duties, and students are feeling neglected. Authoritarian attitudes still persist among some teachers and administrators, and are resented by students.

In most countries students are chronically short of money while living amid increasing affluence. In purely economic terms they do form a large underprivileged proletariat. They no longer accept the traditional view that students should put up with hardships because they are privileged in other ways, or will earn more later, or because the rewards of scholarship are sufficient compensation.

Student salaries

To study is no longer regarded as a special privilege. Students know that the state needs them more than they need the state. Hence the attraction of the syndicalist demand that students should be paid salaries as 'intellectual workers'.

In all these educational grievances the militant students are obviously speaking for a considerable number of their fellows. This is why they can get support in the streets, and it helps to account for the breakaway 'anti-universities' which are cropping up in the United States, Germany and London. They are attempts to recreate the older idea of a university as a small community of teachers and scholars pursuing inquiry together.

But in wider matters, too, the militant students articulate some generalized feelings of their generation. The two main threads that run through the protest movement are concern about the power and dignity of the individual in modern society, and disillusion with governments and political parties. In both threads there is an element of strong moral concern that is shared by students who do not necessarily want revolution or even demonstrations. It is, of course, a familiar characteristic of youth to prefer abstract ideas and moral postures to practical politics. But the feeling that no political party is worth supporting, that party politics are altogether unreal, that governments themselves are increasingly powerless, seems to be increasing.

One sign of this wider rejection is the swing away from the natural sciences reported by the Dainton Committee in Britain earlier this year, and also detectable in some other western countries. The Wilsonian idea that what youth wants is the white heat of the technological revolution seems wide of the mark. To a large extent the protest movement expresses distrust of the technological revolution.

And this distrust is not among people excluded from its benefits. It comes from the most intelligent and in part the most affluent section of the population. Many of the sociology students in the protest movement have voluntarily abandoned the natural sciences and all the security and material rewards they would have brought. They no longer see science as the light of the future guiding men out of superstition and poverty to greater wealth and wisdom. They see it as developing a power of its own – the sort of power that drives governments to build space rockets and supersonic aircraft instead of houses and schools. They look for answers not in more science but in better understanding of social and human relationships and of the individual himself.

Probably student unrest is not wholly unrelated to the casual and seemingly pointless vandalism with which less educated and less organized youths express their frustration, alienation and general hostility in our cities. In a less articulate way they are asking some of the same questions about the meaning of life. There are no wars to be fought, no external threats to meet, and few frontiers to be explored. The climax of human achievement and ambitions is the suburban house, the family, and the car. Most nations can no longer risk competing for territory or diverting attention from domestic problems with foreign adventures. Inevitably they turn in on themselves.

Like it or not, students have now become conscious of their power. They have also come to feel that it is fashionable to use it. In many universities in Britain there are groups of students looking round for issues on which to confront the authorities. It is the action that counts, issues are secondary. One must not fall behind the times – or the French.

At some point this imitative element will fade away. Perhaps students who have been pressing for a share of the administrative power will also discover just how incredibly boring it can be to sit on committees. The student body changes all the time. It cannot easily establish itself as a consistent political power in the nation.

But even allowing for all the factors that may be transitory, we are likely to be faced for a long time with some of the more fundamental elements in the protest movement – a very large and articulate student body, an educational crisis, and the political alienation of a substantial part of the student generation.

DISCUSSION POINTS

1   In your opinion should students who are supported by public money have their grants withdrawn if they spend some of their time protesting instead of working?

2   Have students in this country got genuine grievances? If so, what is the best way for them to improve their situation – by violent demonstration, through peaceful protest, or by greater participation in the existing democratic set-up?

3   Should students have a greater say in what they are taught?

4   Are student grants high enough?

5   Is a college or university education a special privilege or should students be regarded as 'intellectual workers' and paid salaries accordingly?

6   For some students, says Richard Davy, action is more important than issues. Are the extreme revolutionaries really concerned with improving society or simply with the apparent 'glamour' of being revolutionaries?

Patrick Seale and Maureen McConville
The French Revolution 1968

from *French Revolution 1968*, Penguin 1969

Of all the militant student agitations of recent years those in France in May 1968 came nearest to achieving what the more extremist student leaders hope for – the overthrow of the existing government leading to a social revolution. The following passage, taken from *French Revolution 1968* by Patrick Seale and Maureen McConville, describes some of the events of that May and explains why they happened.

Students are far better equipped for insurrection than most adults recognize. They have time to plot; freedom from bread-and-butter constraints; the confidence of their class and education; faculty buildings in which to meet; above all, *energy* – the energy to march from one end of Paris to the other, to fight all night, and still be fit enough to draft, print and distribute a revolutionary tract before dawn. Adults are no match for such demonic stamina.

In the week from Monday, May 6, to Monday, May 13, the students' revolt changed fundamentally in character: from pranking and street brawls it became a mass insurrection. In that week the revolutionary leaders first took command – however tenuously – of large-scale forces, and demonstrated their gifts for mobile strategy, spreading disorder across the face of Paris and tying down tens of thousands of police. The revolutionaries set the pace, they seized the initiative, forcing a baffled government into error after error. Within the first twenty-four hours the movement spread to provincial universities, provoking a rash of demonstrations and strikes at Aix-en-Provence, Bordeaux, Caen, Clermont-Ferrand, Dijon, Grenoble, Montpellier, Nantes, Rouen, and

Toulouse. In that first unforgettable week the most striking quality of the student explosion was joy. Later the revolt was to degenerate into pathos and squalor, but at this early stage, whatever the cold plotting of some of the leaders, it all seemed wild youthful exhilaration, full of a crazy Utopian hope. There was a spontaneous surge of the spirit, expressed in the marvellous claim scrawled on the faculty wall: 'Here, imagination rules!' The most cynical adults were moved. Public sympathy welled up, enclosing the rebels in a protective cocoon so that they became invulnerable. The authorities only blackened themselves by striking at them.

Seething from the police 'rape' of the Sorbonne on Friday, and from the weekend sentences imposed on four young men, four to five thousand student demonstrators responded to the call of Jacques Sauvageot, the UNEF leader, to turn out from nine a.m. on Monday morning. But nothing much happened before lunch, except for a spirited march around the Latin Quarter, marked by small clashes with the police and the chanting of new slogans: 'Roche resign!' 'Professors not cops!' Cohn-Bendit was otherwise occupied. Singing the *Internationale* and with clenched fists raised, he and the other Nanterre troublemakers, accompanied by their lawyer, reported early that morning to the Sorbonne for their 'trial' by the university's disciplinary council. The ushers wanted them in one at a time. They refused, saying they would go in together, or not at all. The authorities gave way. The council – the seven deans of the Paris faculties, supported by two jurists – sat until one p.m. The meeting was lively. 'We had four hours of fun,' Cohn-Bendit said laconically as he left the Sorbonne to join the day-long demonstration in the street.

There was no checking the headlong flight of events. For the first time since the Algerian War, dozens of university teachers marched with the students. Support came also from hundreds of teenage militants mobilized for the occasion by the school action committees, the CALs. A procession formed after lunch outside the new Science Faculty on the Quai St Bernard, and headed towards Notre Dame along the river, growing all the time and derisively chanting: '*Nous sommes un groupuscule*' (We are a tiny group) – a reference to the many critics, on the conservative right as in the orthodox Communist Party, who sneeringly dismissed the student protest as the work of a handful of troublemakers. Nowhere along their route, as the marchers turned away from the river towards the Latin Quarter, was there any evidence of public hostility. Here and there their progress was even marked by bursts of clapping from balconies. So far all was peaceful. But at three p.m. the procession, advancing peacefully on the Sorbonne, was surprised by a fierce police charge, which sent it reeling back to the Boulevard St Germain, leaving wounded students lying in the street.

This was the opening engagement in twelve hours of violent and almost continuous skirmishing, the worst rioting Paris had known since the Algeria disorders. It was like a sudden release of aggression after long years of conscientious homework and clean collars on Sundays. Girls displayed as much reckless courage as boys. Masking their faces with handkerchiefs to protect themselves against the clouds of tear-gas, demonstrators set fire to cars, formed human chains to throw up cobble-stone barricades, attacked fire engines with sticks and stones, braving the jets, spat, and screamed, and fought under the savage truncheons of the police. There was an inexplicable element of demented hate in the way ten thousand young people, mostly of good family, pitted themselves against some of the best trained and most ferocious riot police in Europe.

The all-pervasive sweet and acrid tear-gas filled cafés and houses and filtered down into the Métro where, that night, hundreds of passengers rumbling back and forth beneath the Latin Quarter, wept in their trains, first without knowing why, and then sniffing the gas, grinning and giggling in sympathy with the students. It is no accident that the ladies who punch tickets in the underground are the descendants of those who knitted at the guillotine. The insurrectional spirit of Paris is here provided with a highly appropriate home.

Three hundred Red Cross volunteers, linked by radio to their headquarters, braved the flying cobble-stones to carry 150 wounded off the battlefield. Over 450 others, both students and police, were given first-aid on the spot. The night ended with no fewer than 422 arrests.

A pattern of violence had been laid down. Great numbers of young people had learned – in the most practical of schools – the daring techniques of street fighting. Loathing for the police, and for the government which had sent them out, became unquestioned. To the observer, one of the puzzles of the May Revolution is that, from the first day of serious fighting, it was hard to establish at whose door responsibility should be laid: was it the heavy hand of the police which had lit the fuse, or was it, perhaps, the deliberate courting of repression by small groups of hard-headed revolutionary tacticians?

'CRS – SS': this particularly insulting slogan was scrawled on walls and chanted by demonstrators throughout the month of May. It was both unfair and inaccurate: unfair because whatever the charges against the French police, they have nothing in common with Hitler's; and inaccurate because not all French police are CRS (Compagnie républicaine de sécurité), as some students supposed. There are also a uniformed city police force, lots of plainclothes men, and a National Gendarmerie. All these instruments went into action against the student rebels, and not all emerged with nerve and honour intact. There is a great weight of evidence – admittedly largely from student sources – to show that on regrettably numerous occasions, the 'forces of order' lost their heads and were inexcusably brutal, not only in the heat of battle, but to prisoners in their custody, notably in one of the detention centres where large numbers of young people were held, often in extreme discomfort. One early eye-witness account in Paris was that of Dr Le Guen. (In a letter to *Le Monde* of May 9, 1968.) From his window, he saw a score of policemen attack a peaceful and crowded café, knocking people about, using their truncheons freely on faces and shins, and carting off a dozen young men to a police van. One of them, a coloured boy, got into the police van under his own steam, but a quarter of an hour later an ambulance roared up to take him away on a stretcher. There was blood all over his face.

One way and another, May was a trying time for the police. They were ordered by their political masters to quell 'with the utmost vigour' a series of large-scale riots, only to find the government a moment later parleying with the rioters. This seemed to leave them out on a limb, in the chill of public hostility. Not unnaturally they grew restive. Dissatisfied rumblings in the force found expression in statements by the various police unions, pinning responsibility for what they had done squarely on the government. From mid-May onwards there were rumours that the police could not wholly be relied upon for further repression. No doubt to restore their morale, General de Gaulle himself paid them public tribute.

Order in Paris is normally maintained by the *agents de la paix*, used mainly for directing traffic and suchlike, but who can – and do – turn out for riot duty, dressed in long black macs and carrying square shields and wooden truncheons. If they cannot cope, highly trained anti-riot 'intervention companies' are called in, who in street combat wear khaki denims. Both these forces are part of France's 60,000 city and municipal police, controlled in Paris by the Prefecture. If further reinforcements are required, the CRS, run by the Minister of the Interior, can be asked to intervene. They are a nation-wide force, 14,000-strong, deployed in the ten military districts of the country, and used for fighting forest fires and mountain rescue as well as traffic control between cities. In riots they carry round shields and long black rubber truncheons. Finally, in real emergencies, the authorities can throw into battle the 16,000-strong mobile *gendarmerie* controlled by the Army and recognizable by its black jackets, blue trousers with a black stripe, and rifles. To the students they are all *flics*.

Baron Haussmann drove wide, straight boulevards through the populous labyrinth of nineteenth century Paris to provide the Emperor's troops with clear fields of fire in case of insurrection. The result was so to unite the city that now a boulevard is the natural centre for insurrection, as the events of May demonstrated. 'Hard luck, Baron H: game, set and match to the rabble.' (For a new view of Paris, see *Nairn's Paris* by Ian Nairn, Penguin Books, 1968.)

The main weapon on the rabble side was the *pavé* – the cubic French cobble-stone, weighing about three pounds, easily prised from the roadway by determined men. On some battlefields, the demonstrators used pneumatic drills to loosen them. Barricades of *pavés*, as high as a man, were thrown up with incredible speed, providing almost unlimited supplies of ammunition. Some of the worst police casualties were caused by *pavés* received in full face or chest, sometimes thrown from balconies with punishing effect. The police riposte was almost as traditional: the truncheon, the gas grenade, and on rare occasions high-pressure water jets, which can knock a man down or even toss him several yards. The police were able to keep their enemy at bay, thanks to their snub-nosed grenade-throwing guns fired from the hip, with a range of over 150 yards. Two sorts of gas grenade were used: the older CN (Chlora-cetophenone) which produces violent eye and throat irritation, weeping and choking, but is made immediately harmless by water; and the more recent CS (known in France as CB) (O-chloro-benzal-malono-nitrile), first developed in Britain, which has three main advantages over the CN – it provokes nausea, it hangs in the air longer, and its effects are more rather than less disagreeable in damp conditions. CS gas in contact with water can cause nasty skin burns, as many demonstrators found to their cost, when trying to protect their faces with wet handkerchiefs. The police also threw offensive grenades, used extensively for riot control during the Algerian War, which have a blast effect. They make an intimidating noise as thousands of Parisians who lost several nights' sleep can testify.

Professor Francis Kahn, of the Lariboisière Hospital, Paris, who prepared a report for the Russell Tribunal on the use of chemical and biological weapons in Vietnam, pronounced CS gas toxic, on evidence drawn from Vietnam and from laboratory experiments on animals. But it is perhaps significant that he did not publicly renew his charges against CS gas since his Paris press conference on May 13. The case against CS gas was not proved, and the weight of evidence from the severe fighting in Paris did not add up to a conclusive indictment. Even bitter critics of French police brutality were forced to concede that, when used under 'normal circumstances' – that is, in the open air against able-bodied demonstrators – the gas caused no permanent injury. The trouble was that grenades were sometimes tossed into police vans, already crowded with demonstrators under arrest, or lobbed through windows into people's houses.

In the week beginning Monday, May 6, the current was running all the way for the students. Pompidou was still talking to the Shah; de Gaulle was silent; and Peyrefitte, the young untried Minister of Education, bungled, throwing away a political career which until that moment had seemed highly promising. It was the week in which Jacques Sauvageot and Alain Geismar, the spokesmen of the students' and teachers' unions, emerged into national prominence, outdistancing in the public eye the real political leaders of the Revolution, and rivalling in glamour even Cohn-Bendit himself. It was a colossal test for these young men. It is not given to many people to lead vast, turbulent demonstrations through Paris, to take at each cross-roads strategic decisions of the first importance, to conduct running negotiations with the police, to decide when to stand and fight, when to give way, when to ignore parleys and let the sheer mass of the human wave behind you carry the day. In that week the movement was at its most respectable: it aroused sympathy, not fear. The student demands at this stage carried no hint of Utopia, nothing disruptive of the social order, nothing which did not seem justified by the unhappy events of the previous few days.

They said they were ready to negotiate with M. Peyrefitte if three requests were first granted them: the withdrawal of the police from the Latin Quarter, the immediate freeing and pardoning of students either sentenced or under arrest, the reopening of the university. Everywhere they found support. Schoolboys in a score of Paris lycées struck in sympathy, staged sit-ins, organized strike pickets, and joined demonstrations.

The Grandes Ecoles themselves, the envied peaks of French élitist technocratic education, abandoned work to join the movement. Liberal professors from Nanterre and the Sorbonne went down into the street to express solidarity with the students. One of the most eloquent appeals for comprehension came from Professor Alain Touraine, the Nanterre sociologist, who had predicted the student explosion, and now sought to steer it into constructive channels. He warned again that there could be no escape from the head-on clash unless repression ceased and the existence of the student movement was accepted. (*Le Monde*, May 11, 1968.)

It was this groundswell which carried 30,000 students on an extraordinary five-hour romp round Paris on Tuesday, May 7 – and at least that number again in a dozen provincial towns. The police in serried ranks surrounded the Sorbonne, closing all approach roads. And so, as their Latin Quarter was in enemy hands, the students went elsewhere, looping round the handsome boulevards in an extravagant, joyful, 25-kilometre ramble. It seemed that night as if Paris was theirs. Chanting '*Nous sommes un groupuscule*', they assembled in their thousands under their red and black flags, charged the thinly guarded Concorde bridge, hurled defiance at the staid, reproving *Figaro*, and swarmed up the Champs-Elysées to the Arc de Triomphe, where with fists raised they sang the *Internationale* on the tomb of the Unknown Soldier. Somehow their leaders brought these untidy thousands home to the Latin Quarter across the river without a single clash with the police. It was only there, after midnight, that finding the police still occupying 'their' home ground, excitement and a sense of triumph broke out in a series of wild skirmishes, producing the now routine crop of destroyed cars, injured, and arrests. But on the whole it had been the students' day, a demonstration of discipline, power, and reasonableness.

This was the high point of public support for the student revolt. On May 8 the French public opinion poll, IFOP, reported that four-fifths of Parisians were in favour of the students. At this early stage the great mass of the bourgeoisie itself seemed won over. The middle classes – parents of the demonstrators – were more incensed at police repression than concerned at the assault the students were mounting on the bourgeois state. More predictably a group of leading left-wing intellectuals, including Jean-Paul Sartre and Simone de Beauvoir, formed a Committee of Support for Student Victims of Repression. Five French Nobel Prize winners – Messrs Jacob, Kastler, Lwoff, Mauriac, and Monod – sent General de Gaulle a telegram pleading for an amnesty for the students and the reopening of the university. But the General was silent.

Never in those crucial days, before the student revolt spread to the workers, did the government by word or gesture suggest that it had grasped what the explosion was about. Sixty thousand students throughout France had demonstrated on the Tuesday, and yet at Wednesday's Cabinet meeting Peyrefitte dismissed the crisis as the work of 'specialists in agitation and elements foreign to the university'. He did no better at the emergency debate in the National Assembly that afternoon – the first time in the history of the Fifth Republic that the Chamber, largely by-passed by de Gaulle's style of government, had been called upon to pronounce on an issue of such burning topicality. The Minister could only see the handful of *enragés* – anarchists, Castroists, and nihilists – who were at the bottom of the trouble. He did not recognize that the movement had mushroomed beyond them. His obtuseness must be counted a contributory factor to the savage fighting which lay ahead. 'If order is restored,' he said, 'all is possible; if it is not, nothing is possible.' These were not sentiments to appease the students. Gaullists as well as Opposition spokesmen took the Minister to task, but, although showing great strain, he gave no ground. 'Youth is not always right,' the Socialist leader, M. Mitterrand, declared, 'but a society which mocks at youth, misunderstands it and strikes at it is always wrong.' The most moving expression of concern, mirroring many an adult's disarray, came from a former Gaullist minister, M. Edgard Pisani: 'When faced by my son and his friends, I sometimes have to keep silent, or even to lie, because I am at a loss to answer their questions. . . .' Even the Communists, who had watched the growth of the extremist movement on their left with dismay and indignation, denouncing the *enragés* as 'leftist adventurists', now reluctantly rallied to their support, joining their voice to the clamour for an amnesty. But for General de Gaulle a return to order was the first priority.

All was now set for the clash on the terrible night of May 10–11, which echoed round the world and cracked wide open the complacent façade of Gaullism. Confronted with a deeply frustrated, deeply provoked student body, barely contained by its own leaders, the government stumbled from brutal reaction to incomprehensible inaction. It must be held largely responsible for the subsequent disorders, whatever part extremists played in courting a show-down. Thursday, May 9, was probably the last occasion when an intelligent and imaginative gesture by M. Peyrefitte might have drawn the fuse. On Wednesday night 20,000 students had marched in peace from one boulevard to another in the Latin Quarter, guilty of nothing worse than a few catcalls directed at the massed police standing guard at the approaches to the Sorbonne. There was no blood-letting. The student leaders, Jacques Sauvageot and Alain Geismar, had shown considerable courage in restraining their more combative followers and giving the order to disperse. A word of appreciation on Thursday from Peyrefitte might have brought a de-escalation. All morning Rector Roche and his faculty deans anxiously debated the explosive situation. At lunch-time they made public their decision: to reopen the university and resume work. UNEF's response was immediate: the students' strike would go on until their three conditions had been met – the freeing of all students under arrest, the end of court proceedings against them, and the withdrawal of the police. SNESup, the teachers' union, also decided to continue its strike. That afternoon the doors of the Sorbonne remained locked and under police guard. The Minister gave no instructions to open them. He explained his firmness in a communiqué later that night: some of the student leaders, he said, had threatened to 'occupy' the Sorbonne and hold day and night meetings there, on the problems of the university; this could not be considered a return to work and calm; the Sorbonne would remain closed. Thus the Minister torpedoed the gesture made by the Rector earlier in the day. Shortly before midnight the council of the university issued a statement expressing confidence in Rector Roche. The opportunity for appeasement had passed.

On the student front the situation now entered a more political phase. The government's intransigence gave the revolutionary hard core the opportunity to reoccupy the front of the stage and seize the initiative from the more moderate student leaders. That same Thursday night the Jeunesse communist révolutionnaire – the Trotskyist political faction behind Cohn-Bendit – called a mass meeting at the Salle de la Mutualité, at which, for perhaps the first time since the beginning of the crisis, the extremists publicly showed their hand. So the revolt crossed the frontier from student agitation to political challenge. More than three thousand students packed the hall in an atmosphere of feverish revolutionary ardour. Mobilized by the Trotskyists, representatives of left-wing student groups from Italy, Belgium, Holland, Western Germany, and Spain mounted the platform to express solidarity with their French comrades. The applause was thunderous. Cohn-Bendit was the star of the evening. 'There will be no lectures so long as a single student remains in jail,' he cried. Both Nanterre and the Sorbonne would be taken over by the students as soon as they were opened. So much for tactics. The strategy was laid down by Ernest Mandel, the Belgian member of the three-man unified secretariat which rules over the world Trotskyist movement. The students' struggle, he declared, 'must open out into the general struggle of the working class for a socialist revolution'. Earlier that day a meeting had taken place between UNEF and France's leading trade union bosses, Georges Séguy of the CGT and Eugene Dèscamps of the CFDT, together representing over two million workers. They met to discuss the conditions for joint student-worker union action. It was a first tentative step towards Mandel's revolutionary target. The Night of the Barricades, May 10–11, 1968, has passed into history, one of those tragic and glorious episodes which go to make up France's rich revolutionary tradition. It was a political event of first-class importance in the life of a generation – that born after, say, 1940. Seen from a distance, it may seem only one more disturbance in a disorderly month, an accidental break in the smooth graph of Gaullist rule. But for the thousands who were there that night, who felt the fear and the joy and the delirious solidarity, it will go on reverberating with the emotional power of a first love affair. As with all truly revolutionary moments, its ultimate consequences may not be visible for years.

It all began with the teenagers, at least five thousand of them, their blood up. '*Libérez nos camarades!*' This was the cry, as they marched, red and black flags flying, into the Place Denfert-Rochereau, a vast untidy crossroads, near Montparnasse, with at its centre the old stone Lion de Belfort. From the Lion, high above the crowd, the schoolboy leaders of the Comités d'action lycéens (CALs) worked them up with all the skill and the oratory of seasoned politicians. They were waiting at the rendezvous set by UNEF and SNESup for the great demonstration planned as the students' and teachers' riposte to the government's refusal to give way. And they were early. Since December 1967 – in a bare five months – the CALs had grown (especially in Paris) into a formidable left-wing pressure group, largely under JCR inspiration. They represented the rapid spread of radical ideas to a whole generation of pre-university age, stamping the May Revolution with a gay, teenage freshness. As they waited in the sunshine at Denfert-Rochereau, their leaders sang out the great themes of schoolboy militancy: freedom for political action in the lycée, recognition by the school authorities of the CALs, a share for the pupils in the running of their schools. These boys and girls were the sappers preparing to dynamite the old barracks of French secondary education.

At last the elder brothers and sisters appeared and the teenagers were soon merged in a great crowd, perhaps 15,000-strong. It was at that moment, about 6.30, that word reached the student leaders of new conciliatory proposals from M. Louis Joxe, the acting premier. He offered the immediate withdrawal of police from the Latin Quarter, permission for the students to hold a meeting there that night, and the reopening of the Sorbonne on Saturday. These proposals were put to the crowd. Their answer was a great roar of '*Libérez nos camarades!*' The government's gesture had come too late. Student opinion had hardened. And so the vast gathering moved off towards the near-by Santé Prison where the students thought their comrades were held. Massed police kept them away from the prison walls, but hands reached out from barred windows to wave to them. Arms linked and wearing an assortment of crash helmets, a front rank of hard-core militants strained to contain the crowd and steer it towards the Maison de la Radio, the great circular temple of the French state broadcasting system on the Right Bank of the Seine.

But motorcycle couriers brought news that all the bridges across the river were blocked by police vans parked bumper to bumper. The demonstration, deprived of its target, swept down the Boulevard St Germain on the Left Bank; here again its progress was barred by strong forces of police forcing it ineluctably up the Boulevard St Michel towards the Sorbonne. It was as if the authorities had chosen to risk battle on the students' own ground in the Latin Quarter. The leaders met for hurried consultations. After a week of mounting frustration, they could not propose leading their restive troops back to Denfert-Rochereau: they would not have been followed. Like a flash the order went out: 'The Quarter must be ours at whatever cost!' Immediately, as if obeying some profound mob instinct, the demonstrators fanned out through the familiar labyrinth of student Paris, like guerrillas on their home terrain. On every alleyway and approach road leading to the university, the police found themselves confronted with rebel troops, who like busy termites, started tearing up gratings and traffic signs and burrowing down through the tarmac to the *pavés*. No order was sent out, but perhaps at first from a feeling of exposure, perhaps because, as they waited, the students had nothing better to do, barricades sprang up. On such a dispersed front, there can be no certainty about what exactly happened, but the first barricade – a makeshift thing of overturned cars and assorted débris – was seen at about 9.15 in rue Le Goff, a stone's throw from the southern wall of the Sorbonne. Before the night was out, there were at least sixty, some of them formidable constructions of piled *pavés*, so swiftly and yet neatly built that the belief has spread that young workers came to the aid of the students. Thus has that night entered revolutionary legend: the barricades, an ancient symbol of insurrection here revived, brought about the marriage of intellectuals and workers of which revolutionaries dream.

As news reached the students that the police had called up heavy reinforcements, the throwing up of barricades became more feverish. Building sites were plundered, hoardings torn down from the walls, scaffolding and barbed-wire piled up, and everywhere cars were tipped on their sides and jammed in among the *pavés*. Anxiety was blotted out by a sort of frenetic joy. They were like men preparing to sell their lives dearly.

Shortly after ten p.m., Rector Roche, in a desperate bid to head off a clash, broadcast an appeal from the Sorbonne to the student leaders, inviting them to meet him there and then. An extraordinary exchange followed, between Vice-Rector Chalin and Alain Geismar, the SNESup spokesman, conducted as publicly as any negotiation in history – over the radio. Radio Luxembourg reporters in mobile radio vans had got hold of the two men and put them on the air. Geismar declared there could be no talks until the arrested students were released and amnestied. The students thus posed a condition which it was not in the power of the university authorities to concede. The impasse seemed total. But hope of a settlement welled up again shortly after midnight when it was learned that Cohn-Bendit, together with a group of teachers and students, were after all locked in session with Rector Roche who, in turn, had been on the telephone to M. Peyrefitte, the Education Minister. These hopes were soon dashed. Cohn-Bendit emerged with the words: 'We told the Rector that what is happening in the street tonight is a whole generation rising against a certain sort of society. We told him blood would flow if the police did not leave the Latin Quarter. We know the demonstrators will stay behind the barricades until our three demands have been met.' At 1.15 it was clear there could be no peaceful way out. The Vice-Rector declared: 'We have tried to negotiate. We have tried by all possible means to avoid the use of force, but the situation is now out of our control. We have failed.' An hour later the first wave of police stormed the first student defences.

The decision to attack was taken by a small group of Ministers and senior Elysée officials who met in virtually permanent session all night. At the centre of these sombre and anxious talks was the acting Premier, Louis Joxe, advised by Christian Fouchet (Interior), Pierre Messmer (Army), Georges Gorse (Information) and the luckless Alain Peyrefitte. From the Elysée came Bernard Tricot, de Gaulle's right-hand man, and Jacques Foccart, believed to be the President's adviser on security and intelligence. The inescapable conclusion is that the government's security advisers orverrode the repeated appeals for leniency made by Rector Roche. (The next day the University Council expressed its unanimous regret that Roche's advice had not been taken.)

After the savagery of that night's fighting there was no going back for the student revolutionaries. The movement had acquired its own terrible dynamic. Drawn by the battle commentaries on the independent radio networks, thousands of young people, many of them workers, raced across Paris to join in. It was a free-for-all on a scale to satisfy every repressed dream. First the riot police volleyed in their gas grenades to stampede the enemy troops, and then charged into the breach to capture the barricades. There was stiff hand-to-hand fighting in the choking air. The wounded fell and could not be rescued. Then, to slow the grinding advance of the CRS, the defenders set fire to their barrages. The thud of exploding petrol tanks could be heard across the river on the Right Bank. Ernest Mandel, the Trotskyist Fourth International leader from Brussels, climbed on to a barricade, gazed at the spectacle of fire and desolation and exclaimed joyfully, in his heavy Belgian accent: '*Ah! comme c'est beau? C'est la Révolution!*' He was watching his own car burning.

The Trotskyist youth group, the JCR, played a prominent part in the struggle. Their mass meeting the previous night, to which Cohn-Bendit and several other student leaders had come, confirmed their position as the leading political faction behind the revolt. Their *service d'ordre* (under the command of Yves Niaudet and an Egyptian Copt, Jean Labib) had guarded the front and the flanks of the demonstration. Now, their leaders, Alain Krivine and Henri Weber, ordered the hard-core militants to split up into small groups and help man the barricades. This front-line role stood the JCR in good stead. Their ultra-sectarian rivals, the FER, fared less well. Some 300 to 400 of their shock troops arrived on the battle-field shortly after midnight in almost military formation; but, at the sight of the barricades, their leaders were seized by doctrinal doubts: this was clearly going to be murder. It was an 'adventurist' enterprise, in which the FER would have no part. Their squad marched off the field to the derisive hoots of the embattled students. FER's defection at the hour of combat will long be remembered.

A small German SDS contingent fought by the side of their French comrades (and French police were seen assiduously taking down the German registration numbers of Volkswagens parked that night in the Latin Quarter), but they were not as numerous as they themselves would have wished. That week two SDS leaders, Rabehl and Semmler, were turned back at Orly Airport, and a busload of German student actors was stopped at the Strasbourg frontier post when border police found in their coach helmets, truncheons, revolutionary tracts, as well as Chinese and Vietcong flags.

Lit by the red glare from the fires and under drifting acrid gas clouds, the battle raged for four hours, as the police – in charge after charge – drove the students from their defences, pinning them into an ever smaller redoubt from which they could escape only by braving the fury of rifle butts and truncheons. Residents of the Quarter, horrified spectators of the savage mopping-up operations, passed food and drink to the insurgents, doused them in water to lay the tear-gas, and took fleeing and bleeding students into their houses, from which only too often they were snatched by the police. One girl, who had not taken part in the demonstrations, was attacked in her room by police, stripped, and driven into the street naked. (Letter to *Le Monde* from M. Daniel Moureaud, May 15, 1968.)

Red Cross volunteers were themselves sometimes felled by truncheons, and their patients dragged from stretchers for further beating.

Boys and girls threw themselves into the fighting with incredible abandon and dedication. To many young and high-keyed spirits, this was the chance to join the heroic revolution of Fanon, Guevara, and Debray, to which they had so long thrilled. This was their Vietnam. There was about the events that night an element of 'cinema', not only in the dramatic settings, but in the great self-consciousness of the young actors. In deadly earnest, they were playing a game of guerrillas, acting out the 'colonial revolution' in the heart of a Western capital. In this war-game, the sinister and terrifying police – masked, goggled, helmeted, clad in gleaming black from head to toe – were cast in the role of evil spirits, initiating the innocent to the cruelty and bestiality of the world. It is at such highly-charged moments that politics bite into the mind. 'De Gaulle assassin!' a thousand young throats cried.

At 4.20 in the morning the ministers gathered at the Interior Ministry, issued a brief defensive communiqué. At 5.30 Cohn-Bendit gave

M

the order for dispersal over the radio. At 6.00, exhausted and unshaven, Louis Joxe, Christian Fouchet, Pierre Messmer, and Jacques Foccart drove to the Elysée to report to President de Gaulle that the insurrection had been crushed. The balance sheet: 367 wounded; 460 taken into custody; 188 cars damaged or destroyed; incalculable quantities of hate.

On Friday, May 10, 1968, Americans and North Vietnamese made their first contacts in Paris, the world's 'peace capital'.

Herbert Marcuse, the German-American philosopher often credited with paternity for the world student revolt, was also in Paris that week-end, taking part in a Unesco conference on Marx. He spoke of the new catalysts for revolution in industrial countries, men living on the fringes of society such as the outcasts of black ghettos – and the students.

On Saturday night, May 11, Georges Pompidou, Prime Minister of France, returned to Paris from Iran and Afghanistan. Burnt-out cars still littered the Latin Quarter after the Night of the Barricades. Barely three hours after his arrival, M. Pompidou addressed the nation. Three minutes later he had, single-handed, reversed the whole current of government policy. Toughness, obstinacy, repression, gave way to sweet understanding. The Sorbonne, he announced, would be freely open from Monday, and the Court of Appeal would pronounce on the jailed students. The clear implications were that the police would be withdrawn and the students released. From any other man, this climb-down would have been a defeat. Pompidou turned it into a personal victory. Luckily for him, he had been out of the country when the disturbances took place, and therefore could not be held responsible for the violent turn they took. Moreover his conciliatory decisions marked him out as the one man in the government who could influence General de Gaulle. *'Pompidou a dit "je",'* L'Express, the French weekly reported, in a sly reference to the Prime Minister's increased authority.

But he was like a man trying to stop an avalanche. At five o'clock that Saturday morning students invaded Strasbourg University, hoisted a red flag, and proclaimed the university's 'autonomy' from the Ministry of Education in Paris. They stockpiled food and set up their own militia while hundreds of schoolchildren came out in their support and distributed tracts to the people of Strasbourg to support the students against police repression. This mutiny was a direct reaction to the street-fighting in Paris, which Strasbourg students had indignantly followed on their transistor radios all night. In Paris on Saturday afternoon a small force of about forty militants of the Mouvement d'action universitaire (MAU) occupied an annex of the Faculty of Letters in the Rue Censier. This was a deliberate insurrectional act. They chose the Censier Annex as it was unguarded, whereas the Sorbonne itself was surrounded by thousands of police. The MAU leadership was agreed that a university building must at all costs be occupied, and a general discussion opened. The debate raged, almost without interruption, for two days and nights, from Saturday night to Monday. It was the first impassioned explosion of talk in the capital. How could the students give new impetus to a movement born in the street? How could the university be transformed so that it could in turn transform society? Thus began, in Paris and the provinces, the wave of 'occupations' and tireless debate which marked the May Revolution, spreading with breakneck speed from university to factory, until industry and the public services were paralysed.

M. Pompidou was too late to stop the link-up between workers and students. That Saturday morning the two most powerful union federations, the CGT and the CFDT, together with the FEN, France's major teachers' federation, called on their members to strike and demonstrate on Monday, May 13, the tenth anniversary of the Algiers putsch which brought de Gaulle to power. It was clear that the protest was intended as a political challenge to the régime, a loaded birthday present for the General.

For all his skill, M. Pompidou on his return that night underestimated the strength of public feeling running against the government. Giving in to the students' demands, as he did, was not enough. The opposition dailies, *L'Humanité* and *Combat*, had rushed out special afternoon editions to shriek their indignation at the violence of police repression. Hundreds of anxious parents whose children were missing were besieging hospitals and police stations. The Revolution had started some hours before Pompidou landed at Orly: it would have to run its course.

The immense demonstration, some 800,000 strong, on Monday, May 13, was a landmark: it marched from the Gare de l'Est across the river to the Place Denfert-Rochereau, a political riposte for the Night of the Barricades. By forcing the unions to strike in their favour, by bringing such hordes into the streets, the student leaders demonstrated once and for all that they were no longer a lunatic fringe *groupuscule*, but a national force. They manged to touch something very profound in the conscience of the country, and here, in the massed ranks of workers and in the countless fluttering banners, was the proof of it. They were proved right and those who had sneered at them at the start were proved wrong. They seemed to speak a language which others understood: their folly suddenly seemed reasonable. 'It was an extraordinary day,' Alain Geismar, the SNESup leader, declared. 'The students left the university ghetto to join the workers who had left the ghetto of the factory. Those who had fought in the street met up with those who had looked on. The workers now joined the struggle.' (J. Sauvageot, A. Geismar, D. Cohn-Bendit, J.-P. Duteuil, *La Révolte Etudiante*, Seuil, 1968, p. 56.) Perhaps recognizing this new force, the authorities kept the police well out of sight.

Geismar, Sauvagoet, and Cohn-Bendit, marching with their arms round each other's shoulders, led the 800,000 taking triumphant precedence over the union bosses, Georges Séguy of the CGT and Eugène Descamps of the CFDT. Way back, buried in the crowd, came the left-wing politicians, François Mitterrand, Guy Mollet, Pierre Mendès-France, Waldeck Rochet. They received no deference from the student organizers; they were firmly kept away from the front of the cortège. The young revolutionaries wanted no one to muscle in on their act, no political party to take them over. As usual it was Cohn-Bendit who most pungently expressed their contempt for the official left: 'The Communist Party? Nothing gave me greater pleasure than to be at the head of a demonstration with all that Stalinist filth in the rear.' To the alarm of their union leaders, many young workers seemed to thrill to the students' slogans. The virus was spreading to the base of the labour force and eating away at the leaders' authority.

This great *journée* was the occasion for the issue of new, more militant directives. 'The strike will go on!' declared Jacques Sauvageot. 'All university buildings will be occupied! Our aim is absolutely free political discussions inside the university, as well as the resignation of the Minister of the Interior and the Prefect of Police.' Cohn-Bendit called for action committees to be set up in every firm and in every area of Paris. For those who knew where to look, the young Trotskyists of the JCR, under their leader Alain Krivine, were there in force. It was they who provided the student police-force, the all-important *service d'ordre*, which gave the massive demonstration its shape; controlled traffic along the route; and which, after the workers had dispersed on orders from their leaders, led a student contingent to an open-air meeting beneath the Eiffel Tower on the Champ de Mars, that ancient parade ground, which during the 1789 Revolution had seen many gatherings of discontented citizenry. And then the students dispersed to the cry of 'Everyone to the Sorbonne!'

Pompidou had kept his promise: the imprisoned students had been released, the police had pulled back from the Latin Quarter, the gates of the Sorbonne stood open. The students surged in and took possession. That was the first night of the Student Soviet – an extraordinary example of primitive communism in the heart of a Western industrial country – which was not to end till their expulsion thirty-four days later on June 16. Fired by the students' example, the workers too struck and occupied, first at an aircraft plant at Nantes on Tuesday, and then like wildfire throughout France. How were these soviets organized, what was the mood of this novel experiment, what has remained? These are some of the questions which the following pages will seek to answer.

Background to Revolution

To live through a revolution is a delirious experience. It is a little frightening, but also exhilarating, to see authority flouted and then routed. In the two or three weeks after the Night of the Barricades, France was in a state of revolution. That is to say, the existing power structure – not only political power, but every sort of power – was challenged, and in some cases overthrown, and an attempt was made, however confused and disorderly, to put another in its stead. Students, workers, active citizens, joined together spontaneously in hundreds of insurrectional committees all over Paris, but also in the provinces. This very widespread revolt against the old forms of established authority was accompanied by an acute and profoundly enjoyable sense of liberation. All sorts of people felt it in all walks of life. A great gust of fresh air blew through dusty minds and offices and bureaucratic structures. This throwing off of constraint, this sense of relief was the authentic stamp of the Revolution, the proof that the changes being wrought were really of revolutionary proportions.

Quite suddenly, and for a few precious days, the French, whose normal life is bound by many petty regulations, enjoyed the pleasures of a primitive anarchistic society. It was a society without policemen, with everyone his own traffic cop. In spite of the vexations of life, of the strike, and the drying up of petrol pumps, men will look back on that period and remember it with joy.

The most striking feature of those days was the sight of people talking to each other – not only casual exchanges, but long intense conversations between total strangers, clustered at street corners, in cafés, in the Sorbonne of course. There was an explosion of talk, as if people had been saving up what they had to say for years. And what was impressive was the tolerance with which they listened to each other, as if all those endless dialogues were a form of group therapy. Many French men and women woke up to the fact that their relations with each other had been far too stiff and suspicious, far too unfraternal. It seemed as if the system were wrong: children not speaking freely to their parents, employees touching their caps to the bosses, the whole nation standing to attention before the General and his vision of France.

General de Gaulle's decade of rule is doubtless among the major causes of the May outburst. His paternalism, the control he has exerted over information, the cant and pomp of his style of government, irritate and do not impress the young. They run counter to the irreverent, sceptical, iconoclastic spirit of the age. But de Gaulle is not alone to blame. The explosion was a reaction to the way power has been exercised in France, not only since de Gaulle but since Napoleon – and at every level.

More than most countries, and certainly more than Britain, America, or Western Germany, France is burdened with a centralized, profoundly hierarchical, government bureaucracy. All decisions, even footling ones, are made in Paris. The provinces fret and fume and send memoranda to the distant ministry. Everywhere the petty bureaucrat sits, passing up the dossier to his hierarchical superior, jealously exercising his own limited authority according to the rule-book. 'Napoleon is at last dead, and the longest reign in French history is over,' a commentator in *Le Monde*, Gilbert Cesbron, wrote after the events of May. (*Le Monde*, June 26, 1968.)

But the rigidities of government service are also characteristic of French professional life. At the top of most professional trees sits a mandarin – or a '*grand patron*' as the French sometimes say – behaving like a prince, delegating neither authority nor perks. This may be something of a caricature, but it was on the whole true that before the great shake-up of May, the channels of advancement in very many walks of life were blocked by red-tape, outworn tradition, and by men who were there for life. It was against all these mandarinates in universities, factories, the trade unions, and the professions, that the revolution released a flood of impatience and defiance. No authority was spared. Wherever in the routine of daily life orders were given and were expected to be obeyed, someone got up to challenge the system.

The revolt, then, was directed against the way French society is organized. To this extent it was a specifically French phenomenon. But it may also turn out to be the first outburst against the streamlined tyranny of an advanced Western state. If this is true, it has a more general significance. In the last fifteen-odd years, France has attempted to get into big-time international competition. The scramble to modernize, after centuries of protectionism, disturbed patterns of life, as did the consumer goods which began to flood the French market. All the workers wanted more of them, a bigger share of the cake; but some hated the harsh boring discipline of the assembly-line and regretted the old craftsman's independence; others found jarring and distasteful the brisk, highly competitive chromium-plated world sold by the advertising jingles. Labour relations in French industry tend to be primitive by British or American standards. Skilled workers, clerks, junior managers wanted more information about what was going on in their works, they wanted a share in the decisions which affected them directly, they wanted stronger and more active union leadership. All these grievances, and a thousand others, fed the explosion of May.

The most original and creative phase of the Revolution was the last three weeks of May, from the Night of the Barricades to de Gaulle's prodigious recovery on May 30. It was then that a new political vocabulary emerged, drawing the crowd into action as allies of the young revolutionary leaders. It was then that insurrectional committees sprang up, embodying the thirst for decentralization as well as the urge to run one's own affairs, which lay at the root of the revolt. From the start of their protest movement, the revolutionaries preached 'direct action' as opposed to negotiation. Now the slogan was 'direct democracy' as opposed to the classical delegation of powers within a parliamentary system. Both in direct action and in direct democracy was present the notion of 'permanent contestation' – the view that the bourgeois state and all its institutions must be subject to constant harassment and questioning. Nothing was taken for granted. The 'contestation' could equally well take the form of mobbing a professor, of 'occupying' a faculty, of defying the power of the state by a street demonstration, of locking a factory manager into his office.

Everywhere, from one end of France to another, 'action committees' were spontaneously formed at grassroots level, forums of debate as well as of decision. They were the translation into practical (but often impractical) terms of the twin notions of direct action and direct democracy. These action committees were conceived as the agents of revolutionary change. They were to be the forerunners of a totally new type of society, in which everyone had the right to talk and the right to share in decision-making. These committees – of which at least 450 were set up in those three weeks of May, with widely different functions and membership – were the most characteristic expression of the Revolution. They justified the claim that new and original 'power structures', new revolutionary channels of authority, were merging. The revolutionaries, in their enthusiasm, used such terms as *structures parallèles* and *double pouvoir*.

To many, these ideas and the forms they took seemed deliriously novel. This was not so. There were echoes in the May revolt of Russia, of the 1918 Revolution in Germany, of Spain, and Cuba (indeed, some naïve but ardent spirits are said to have put through long-distance telephone calls to Moscow and Havana to seek advice on how to proceed). Above all, the revolutionaries were inspired by the history of France, by the mood and architecture of Paris, by the memories of violent upheaval just below the surface of French consciousness. The action committees, for example, formed in the twenty *arrondissements* of Paris, were the direct heirs of the committees of *sans-culottes* which ran the forty-eight Sections of Paris in 1790. Both then and now, these were committees of active and militant citizens. They were also the place where systematic indoctrination in the aims and jargon of the Revolution took place. In 1789, the wine shops were another potent channel of communication for revolutionary ideas. It was here that the *menu peuple* gathered to gossip and exchange news. In 1968 this was the role played by the pavement discussions and by the cafés on the boulevards of the Latin Quarter, each a nest of insurgents. Many paid the price. Le Luxembourg, for instance, a popular café on the Boulevard St Michel, was stormed by police one wild night. At closing time the manager threw out his hands and said with magnificent aplomb: 'Gentlemen tonight le Luxembourg will not close its doors; it has none left!'

In 1789 pamphleteers and revolutionary journalists used to congregate nightly to acquire the slogans which gave a positive course to the movement. Similarly this year the revolutionary leaders met each night to issue directives for the pamphlets, tracts, street posters, revolutionary journals which played a big part in shaping popular opinion.

Men like Cohn-Bendit, Jacques Sauvageot, and Alain Geismar were undoubtedly an important element in mobilizing the demonstrations, but the crowds which surged through Paris and manned the barricades were far from being passive instruments: their political awareness was of a very high level. Almost any one of them if asked, could have explained what the revolt was about in the 'right' jargon. They had absorbed and adopted the slogans and ideas of the *avant-garde* political groups which triggered off the disturbances. In this they resembled the revolutionary crowds of 1789, fired by the new ideas of 'liberty' and 'the rights of man', who with more or less articulateness knew that what they were after was a change in the forms of executive power. Again, as in 1789, a piece of news, even sometimes only a rumour, could transform a good-humoured, relatively harmless demonstration into a riot of insurrectionary proportions. For example, in the summer of 1789, a peacefully disposed Sunday crowd of strollers in the Palais Royal was galvanized into revolutionary vigour by the news of Necker's dismissal. (See George Rudé, *The Crowd in the French Revolution*, OUP 1959, p. 220.) In the same way, in Paris last June, a report that a schoolboy had drowned in the Seine when fleeing from a police charge sparked off a city-wide cycle of violence. What could be more like the *Journées révolutionnaires* of the first French Revolution – days of revolutionary struggle in which mobs of *sans-culottes* took part – than the three bloody Fridays of May 1968? Much of the vocabulary seemed almost consciously borrowed from the past. Cohn-Bendit and his friends called themselves the *enragés* in tribute to the group of extremists, led by Jacques Roux, Theophile Leclerc, and Jean Varlet, who so influenced the *sans-culottes* in 1793. Almost every Paris newspaper last May described the Sorbonne as the headquarters of the student Commune, the title given to the Paris local government that emerged after the fall of the Bastille. And how often did the Ministry of the Interior denounce the handful of *meneurs*, trouble making leaders straight out of revolutionary history?

DISCUSSION POINTS

1   In a democracy what is the best way to control demonstrations which look like being violent?

2   What do you think of those who say 'Sometimes violent protest is the only way to get things done'?

3   Some people see the great amount of publicity given to student protest by the newspapers and television as contributing to the climate of violence which sometimes prevails. Do you agree?

4   Could something similar to the French Student Revolution occur in this country?

5   Do you think that anarchy – the abolition of formal central government – could ever work?

6   How important in a free society is the right to protest?

PROJECTS

1   Compare the aims and methods of revolutionaries in the past with those of today.

2   Study accounts of a number of successful revolutions and the kinds of society which have resulted. In all revolutions people suffer. From what you read which revolution do you consider brought about the best results?

READING

Manifesto of the Communist Party, K. Marx and F. Engels (Foreign Language Publishing House, 1957). The classic call to arms of the founders of communism.

Revolution From 1789 to 1906, R. W. Postgate (ed.) (Harper Torchbooks, 1962). A collection of revolutionary documents from the first French Revolution to the first Russian Revolution.

The Left in Europe, David Caute (Weidenfeld & Nicolson, 1966). A history of the European radical movement in the nineteenth and twentieth centuries.

The Unfinished Revolution: Russia 1917–1967, Isaac Deutscher (OUP, 1967). How successful was the Russian Revolution of 1917? A leading left-wing historian gives his assessment.

The Diaries of Che Guevara (Penguin, 1968). The diaries of the chief lieutenant of Fidel Castro the revolutionary leader of Cuba. Che died a martyr's death in Bolivia in 1968.

170

Revolution in the Revolution, Regis Debray (Penguin, 1968.) An account (some would say too uncritical) of the revolutionary thought of Fidel Castro and Che Guevara.

The Dialectics of Liberation, David Cooper (ed.) (Penguin, 1968). A group of radical thinkers writing on subjects which range from psychiatry to guerrilla warfare.

Tad Szulc
Freedom cut short in Czechoslovakia

from *The New York Times*, September 1, 1968

At the beginning of 1968 the Czech Communist Party elected a new leadership. It was far more liberal than anything that country had known since it was taken over by communists in 1947. The old, hard-line leaders who took orders from Moscow were deposed, the secret police abolished and censorship of press, radio and television largely removed. A new air of freedom seemed to sweep through the country and people were able to discuss openly what previously they had been frightened to speak of. But to the Russians and to the communist governments of East Germany and Poland the spread of such freedom was seen as a threat. If such ideas spread to their own countries their own tough, restrictive regimes might find themselves openly challenged, even overthrown. Czechoslovakia also stands between the Soviet Union and West Germany, a country which the Russians fear. While the Czechs remain in the Soviet camp the Russians feel much safer. In 1939 the great powers – Britain, Russia and France – stood by while Adolf Hitler's troops marched in to take the country over. Once again, it seemed, Czechoslovakia was to lose her freedom in a power game in which she was no more than a simple pawn. The sad story is summarized in the following passage.

PRAGUE

The spring of 229 days has come to an end in Czechoslovakia.

It was what the Czechoslovak liberals called the 'spring' of political and human emancipation after twenty long years of wintry Communist rule. It began on January 6 with the launching of a 'democratic socialist revolution' by a group of Communist progressives led by a mild and ideologically quiet Slovak named Alexander Dubcek. It came to a clashing end at dawn of August 21 when Soviet tanks and motorized infantry entered Prague to smash the ideas of Czechoslovakia's writers, artists and philosophers.

The 229 days of what a Czechoslovak playwright has called 'The Spring Between Two Winters' was a period of euphoria and an experiment with no precedent in Communist history.

During that long spring, Czechoslovaks discovered the joys of a free press, of public discussion, of free travel abroad and of freedom from fear. They lustily basked in this new freedom, and their leaders prepared legislation to broaden and consolidate this experiment in democracy-within-Communism.

The euphoria was so great that as day followed day, week followed week and month followed month even the most sceptical of Czechoslovaks began to believe that, indeed, the experiment would succeed.

A 'terrible' price
Whether the leaders of this movement – all of them old Communists obviously familiar with Moscow's thinking – shared this belief is not known. But reporting on the negotiations on Moscow that put the final touches to the liquidation of the process of liberalization, Josef Smrkovsky, chairman of the National Assembly, told the nation last Thursday that although 'we knew we would have to pay a price for it, we did not know the price would be so terrible' as the night of August 21 when Soviet and other Warsaw pact troops drove into Czechoslovakia to occupy the country and terminate the ideological defiance of the Kremlin.

At first, the browbeaten leaders returning from Moscow – several of them, including Dubcek, had arrived in the Soviet capital as prisoners of the Russians – sought to convince the shocked and dismayed population that all was not over and that, indeed it would be possible in some way to continue the 'spirit of January' though at a reduced speed.

But in the days that followed the signing of the still-secret Soviet agreement – it is even believed that the Czechoslovak leaders themselves

173

do not have a copy of the document they signed – it has become evident that in a real sense the liberalizing experiment has run its course, at least for the time being, and that there was not very much that could be done about it.

As, little by little, the Prague leaders unveiled to the citizenry the details of the Moscow accord, the Czechoslovaks learned that their free press would be subject to censorship and so would their outspoken radio and television, and that the attempts to form non-Communist political groups would be outlawed.

As the Soviet shifted last week from the tactics of brute force employed in Prague through the presence of nearly 100,000 troops and 1,000 tanks, and in Moscow through psychological pressure on the Czechoslovak delegates bordering on mental torture to the more sophisticated methods of the stick-and-carrot, the Czechoslovak liberals and the millions of their supporters throughout the country were left with no known weapon to counter the new restrictions and controls.

Skilfully playing upon the desire of the Czech leadership to avoid bloodshed and see the tanks taken out of Prague's streets into the surrounding countryside, the Russians made it clear that their forces would leave the city only if and when the Czechoslovaks rapidly and efficiently fulfilled the 'conditions' of the Moscow agreement.

The operative concept in this operation was 'normalization', the dangerously vague word used in the communiqué on the Moscow talks to describe a state of affairs in which the Soviet would end altogether the occupation of Czechoslovakia. It was being invoked at every turn of a cat and mouse game to force the imposition of censorship, to make the students and the hippies of Prague remove the posters and the slogans offensive to the eyes of the Russians and to manoeuvre and to divide the political forces within the Communist party here.

What, then, was left to liberalization?

Czechoslovaks could still travel freely if free travel meant freedom to escape across the border into Austria. But nobody knew how much longer this relative freedom would continue.

The secret police

The secret police – the Soviet and the resurgent Czechoslovak one – was not yet in evidence, although the security services were being reorganized and, inevitably, would make themselves felt sooner or later in the daily lives of the citizens.

The freedom of the streets was losing its ring as people again began withdrawing into silence.

Having been forced by the initial bravery of the Czechoslovak resistance to give up their original plan to install a purely pro-Moscow leadership and having to retain, instead, Dubcek and his associates at least in the nominal direction of the country's affairs, the Russians were avoiding, thus far, open repression and revenge against those who had defied them. But, people fear, this, too, could change.

The years that have elapsed since the last Soviet military intervention in Eastern Europe, the tank-led crushing of the anti-Communist revolt in Budapest in 1956, have evidently brought changes in the thinking of Soviet leaders, who themselves are faced with new political trends of the younger generation.

It was probably a fair guess that Czechoslovakia would not return entirely to the pre-January days and recede again into the silence of strict orthodox Communist controls. What at best could be hoped for was a state of penumbra in which the growth of democratization was arrested, in which most of the specific gains won in the last seven and a half months would be sacrificed, but in which a ray of hope remained that perhaps within a few years as the world and Communist system went on changing elsewhere, the Czechoslovaks could pick up again where they were forced to leave off at dawn on August 21.

After five days of resistance when youths fought tanks with Molotov cocktails, the clandestine radio and television defied the invaders and the nation as a whole rose in defence of its sovereignty, the Czechoslovaks sadly but realistically have to come to terms with the new situation.

History repeats itself

Czechoslovak history seems to repeat itself. In his memoirs, George F. Kennan quoted a dispatch he wrote from Prague in March, 1939, after the entry of Nazi troops into the city. Remarking on the Czechoslovaks' decision not to resist the invaders, he wrote that this national resolve 'perhaps most important of all has preserved for the exacting tasks of the future a magnificent younger generation – disciplined, industrious and physically fit – which would undoubtedly have been sacrificed if the solution had been the romantic one of hopeless resistance rather than the humiliating but truly heroic one of realism'.

Tad Szulc

This was also true of Czechoslovakia in 1968 after the 229 days of the democratic spring.

DISCUSSION POINTS

1　Are Communism and freedom incompatible?

2　Is there no way in which the freedom of countries like Czechoslovakia – small and difficult to defend against great powers – can be guaranteed?

3　Some people have argued that the United States has no moral right to condemn the Russian occupation of Czechoslovakia when they are guilty of the same sort of action in Vietnam – trying to prevent them from freely choosing their own government. Do you agree?

4　When the Nazis entered Prague in 1939 and when the Russians and her allies invaded in 1968 the Czechs did not resist with armed force but showed in other ways that the invaders were not welcome. What is the best form of defence, passive or violent resistance?

5　What do you think of the idea that all countries should disarm and that international law should be made and enforced by the United Nations?

176